THE POISONED ARROW

Also by don Miguel Ruiz Jr.

The Mastery of Life: A Toltec Guide to Personal Freedom

The Seven Secrets to Healthy, Happy Relationships
(with HeatherAsh Amara)

The Mastery of Self: A Toltec Guide to Personal Freedom

*Don Miguel Ruiz's Little Book of Wisdom:
The Essential Teachings*

*The Five Levels of Attachment:
Toltec Wisdom for the Modern World*

*Living a Life of Awareness:
Daily Meditations on the Toltec Path*

THE POISONED ARROW

A TOLTEC GUIDE TO
OVERCOMING
FEAR

DON MIGUEL RUIZ JR.

Hierophant publishing

Copyright © 2025 by don Miguel Ruiz Jr.

All rights reserved, including the right to reproduce this work in any form whatsoever, without permission in writing from the publisher, except for brief passages in connection with a review.

Cover design by Adrian Morgan
Cover art by Shutterstock
Print book interior design by Frame25 Productions

Hierophant Publishing
San Antonio, TX
www.hierophantpublishing.com

If you are unable to order this book from your local bookseller, you may order directly from the publisher.

Library of Congress Control Number: 2025934291

ISBN: 978-1-950253-59-3

10 9 8 7 6 5 4 3 2 1

To all whom I love.

If you practice the Toltec tradition in the way your father or I practice it, then you are killing the tradition. Don't be afraid to practice it in your own way, for it is your journey.
—Madre Sarita

Contents

Introduction   1

1. A Chorus of Voices   19

2. Fear and Awareness   39

3. The Dreaming Mind   65

4. Happiness and Desire   81

5. Unconditional Love and Acceptance   101

6. Trust and Temachia   123

7. Embracing Uncertainty   147

8. The Divided Mind   165

9. Acknowledging Past Trauma   181

10. Letting Go   207

Conclusion   223

Acknowledgments   227

About the Author   229

Introduction

Imagine a man walking through a village when he is suddenly struck by a poisoned arrow. Several friends rush to his side, and one runs off to alert the village doctor, who arrives quickly to remove the arrow and administer an antidote.

"Wait!" orders the man. "Before you remove it, I need to know: Who shot me? Where are they from? Why did they shoot me? Was it a long bow or a short bow?"

The doctor and the man's friends look at each other, puzzled, as clearly the man will die from his wound before these questions can be answered.

This beautiful Buddhist parable has many lessons for us. First, it acknowledges that we will all be wounded at some point in our lives. None of us reach adulthood without experiencing at least one significant emotional wound that impacts us greatly. Second, it points out that many of us prefer to ruminate on our wounds, spending hours, weeks, or even decades trying to figure out the causes of our pain. According to Buddhist teachings, too much abstract speculation can be a dangerous thing, distracting us from the practical tasks that lead to healing. Although intellectual answers may seem to give us a sense of control, ultimately the real task at hand is to simply yank the arrow out.

While I agree with the lessons that Buddhism teaches here, including the importance of removing the arrow quickly, I also believe that while the arrow's tip may leave a painful wound, it is the poison left behind that presents the greatest danger to our well-being. The poison on this arrow is *fear*. Ultimately, fear can infiltrate our hopes, dreams, and personalities, becoming the defining factor in our lives—until, that is, we discover the antidote.

The Poison

Human beings are subject to two kinds of fear. The first is physical: the rush of alertness you feel when you see a deer dart across the highway at night, or a bear foraging for food just feet away from you. Physical fear can be natural and helpful: it produces adrenaline, which elevates your heart rate, increases your oxygen intake, and gives you the temporary boost of energy and focus you need to fight that bear or run for your life. In evolutionary terms, physical fear is *adaptive*: a trait that makes it more likely that you will survive and thrive in your environment. Although the sensation of physical fear may be unpleasant, there's no doubt that it helps us in true survival situations.

Physical fear is associated with our body's fight, flight, or freeze response, and it is hardwired into us to ensure our survival. Throughout most of human history, this was the dominant form of fear that people experienced. Far from being a hindrance, our capacity to feel physical fear allowed our species to survive and evolve over hundreds of thousands of years.

I often think about how nice it would be if we felt *only* physical fear—if we could go about our days feeling completely calm and secure, except for those extremely rare moments when we needed to respond to an unexpected physical threat in our environment. In our relatively safe and comfortable modern world, you might go a long time without feeling any fear at all. Yet, for better or for worse, we humans are also prone to another type of fear, and that's the type I'll be addressing in this book.

Psychological fear covers a range of emotions, from social anxiety to feelings of unworthiness to worries about scarcity that have nothing to do with our survival. We fear that others will not like us, that we will fail to reach a goal we hold dear, or that a decision we made in the past has control over our future; we fear that our future happiness will be compromised, that we will lose something or someone we cherish, or that something about us is fundamentally bad, flawed, inferior, or unlovable.

Psychological fear is so prevalent today that many people live in a nearly perpetual state of fear and don't even realize it. Some will deny this. But if you look closely, you'll find that the fear is there, lurking just beneath the surface and controlling their actions and reactions. Many fear they won't succeed financially, or experience contentment and joy in their relationships, or find perfection in their physical appearance. While they may tell themselves that they are free, their actions tell a different story, and this includes those instances when the mind justifies the actions as "this is what I really want" rather than "I'm doing this because I am afraid."

From this perspective, we can see that psychological fear is a corrosive thread that runs through many aspects of our lives. Sadly, the physical responses to psychological fear versus physical fear are often very similar: a racing heart; sweaty palms; a stomach twisted in knots. Our bodies endure an inordinate amount of physical stress that, over the course of a lifetime, can have harmful consequences. Even though we have more resources than our ancestors could have ever dreamed of, and access to modern medicines and technologies that keep us physically safer than any previous generation, we nevertheless spend our days in a state of sustained, elevated stress.

Left unchecked, psychological fear can lead us to make strict agreements about who to trust, where to go, and how to live. It can cloud our judgment, causing us to overestimate the dangers we face, while underestimating our own ability to handle them. It can limit our possibilities in life, as we opt out of situations that we perceive as threatening, regardless of whether or not they truly are. It can impact our relationships, as we attempt to shelter our loved ones and then become frustrated when they question why or rebel against these so-called dangers. Long after the arrow has been removed, the poison of psychological fear lingers, turning us into prisoners of our own minds.

The marketing and advertising industries have long harnessed the power of psychological fear for financial gain. Through ads and stories they suggest that we will miss out on pleasure, connection, beauty, and ease if we don't buy what their clients are selling. Many companies reap huge profits by stoking our fears of crime, violence, or invasion by a nefarious "other." We buy products to feel safer, to feel more in control. Whether that safety is real or only perceived doesn't matter—for the moment, clicking that "buy now" button offers a simple, accessible way to quiet the fear that something could go wrong or somehow be vaguely better. By tapping into our reserves of fear, adept marketers can persuade us that we will regret *not* taking action immediately—never mind whether that action is a beneficial one or not. For peace of mind, we follow their lead.

Our culture in general prods us to endlessly pursue financial goals, acquire objects that convey our status, or attain some special standing in the community, administering a massive dose of stress. This may motivate us in the short term but ultimately drains our inner resources.

For all of the fear present in the culture at large, much of the damage is woefully self-inflicted, and on a small, intimate scale, done by people close to us. Many of us use fear as a tool to bond with others—for example, by indulging in harmful gossip and building ourselves and our coconspirators up at the expense of someone else. Although this kind of gossip may make us feel close with others initially, it inevitably leads us to mistrust them later (*Are they talking about me now?*), and it always creates division in the wider community. We're going to talk a lot in this book about the power of words, and how we have the opportunity to stoke or alleviate fear by noticing the source of these many messages vying for our attention.

It is for these reasons that in my family's Toltec tradition we say that fear is the great poison, causing everything from minor disagreements between friends and family to major conflicts like world wars. It is not hyperbole when I say that psychological fear is the root cause of all greed, envy, gossip, anger, and virtually every harmful action that humans take against one another and the planet. Not only does fear keep us from experiencing joy and peace in our lives, but I believe it to be the greatest threat to humanity's long-term survival on this planet. I don't say this lightly. If you look closely, you'll see that fear is at the root of every war and threat of war; fear drives the greed that is taxing the resources of our planet; fear prevents the wealthiest of us from helping those who are less fortunate; and on a personal level, fear is the greatest obstacle to personal freedom, or what other spiritual traditions may call self-realization.

While the challenges facing humanity are numerous, the Toltec tradition also teaches that in order to change the world we must be willing to look within and change ourselves. In fact, we cannot change others. This is impossible. I am the only one who can change me, and you are the only one who can change you. We also recognize that at the deepest level, all humans have their own answers—but sometimes we need a guide to help us find them. This book, along with all the teachings in my family's tradition, endeavors to act as a guide to help you rediscover what you already know: that there is an antidote to this poison of psychological fear.

If you've read any of my other books, or my family's books, you'll know that my work is deeply informed by Toltec culture. Growing up, I was surrounded by incredible examples of ancient Toltec wisdom brought to life: my father, don Miguel Ruiz, and my grandmother, Madre Sarita, a well-known *curandera*, or faith healer, both instilled in me the precious gifts that Toltec teachings have to offer. To make sure that we're all on the same page, before we go further, I'll say a little more about my Toltec ancestors and some of the key concepts that we will return to throughout this book.

What the Toltecs Can Teach Us

The Toltec civilization thrived in the region now known as south-central Mexico, reaching its peak one thousand to three thousand years ago. The Toltecs were renowned for their advanced society, which placed great emphasis on human perception as it relates to spiritual development. They viewed themselves as artists—in fact, the word *Toltec* means "artist" in the Nahuatl language. While they did indeed create remarkable works of painting, sculpture, and architecture, including the impressive Pyramids of the Sun and the Moon near present-day Mexico City, the Toltec concept of artistry extends far beyond these traditional forms. In the Toltec worldview, every human being is an artist, and the art we are all creating is the story of our lives.

One of the core spiritual insights of the Toltecs is that the human mind is dreaming all the time.

We all experience life through the filter of our individual consciousness; as such, the reality we see in the outside world mirrors our personal beliefs. We call this the Personal Dream. Your Personal Dream may be beautiful or ugly, pleasant or frightening, depending on your beliefs, your thoughts, and the conscious or unconscious agreements you make.

The combination of every single Personal Dream makes up what we call the Dream of the Planet, or the collective dream we all share. The Dream of the Planet is an amalgamation of all our Personal Dreams. This collective dream is shaped by the agreements we make on a massive scale: for example, the agreement to recognize some people as "owners" of land or natural resources, to recognize certain pieces of paper as valuable currency, or to believe in a certain god or follow a particular religion. While agreements like these can be helpful in forming a working society, it's important to remember that the beliefs behind them have no outside validation beyond the mind.

Another core concept in Toltec spirituality is the *nagual*, a Nahuatl word that has two meanings. The first meaning is roughly equivalent to the modern English understanding of "shaman," or someone who held the role of spiritual teacher in our native community. In that sense, I am a nagual, or shaman, in my family's lineage. I studied for many years under my father and grandmother, and was bestowed this title by them upon completion of my training. This meaning of the word *nagual* is relatively easy to understand.

The other meaning of the word *nagual* is more esoteric. As a living being, I am filled with nagual, and so are you. In this usage of the word, *nagual* refers to the life force energy that is present in all of us, and that is also responsible for making rivers flow and flowers bloom. Comparing this to other spiritual traditions, the word *nagual* is reminiscent of terms like *chi*, *prana*, and *wakan*. The nagual is the energy that gives life to all beings and is equally present in all beings. Whether you are a mouse or a lion, a king or a peasant, you carry this precious nagual inside you as long as you live. As you will see in this book, learning to recognize and honor the nagual in yourself and in all beings is central to overcoming the poisonous effects of fear.

The Antidote

In the pages that follow, I'll share several Toltec techniques for recognizing psychological fear in its many forms, examining the ideas, beliefs, and past experiences that feed them, and harnessing the courage of the Toltec warrior to rise above the fear-based beliefs that are keeping you trapped in a metaphorical prison. You'll learn how to rewrite the fear-based agreements you've made with yourself and with life, release unhelpful beliefs that are at the source of many of these fears, and draw on Toltec practices for staying present and aware in the midst of discomfort and uncertainty.

My hope is that by the end of this book you will not only see psychological fear as a poison, but also a gift. When I say psychological fear can also be a gift, that surprises some people—but fear can show us where we need to do more inner work in our quest for personal freedom. This is the unique (and perhaps only) benefit of psychological fear.

As my father likes to say, it's one thing to read a recipe, and another thing to cook the dish. This book is not just a collection of philosophical ideas, but a road map containing practical exercises and meditations designed to help you live peacefully in a world that can sometimes seem scary, unpredictable, and overwhelming. By doing the exercises and engaging with the self-reflections in this book, instead of just reading about them, you can forge a new relationship with fear that will utterly transform your life.

Psychological fear is a poison that fuels the beliefs that keep us from living in a state of internal peace and making our lives the masterpieces of art that my Toltec ancestors envisioned. Questioning these beliefs and changing the behaviors associated with them can be difficult, even emotionally painful, but once this discomfort has passed, the real healing can begin.

As you begin to recognize your psychological fears, the awareness alone can bring you a new sense of calm, clarity, playfulness, and joy. You'll discover inner wells of strength and creativity you never knew were there. Relationships will become more genuine and fulfilling as you learn to connect with others from a place of authenticity rather than a place of fear or insecurity. Even the outside world, with its many perils, will seem to change, as it is ultimately a reflection of your Personal Dream — one that is no longer clouded by unnecessary fear.

Most important, as psychological fear loosens its grip on you, you'll begin to recognize yourself as the artist of your own life. Your life will transform from a series of fear-based reactions rooted in unexamined, limiting personal beliefs and assumptions into a masterpiece of your own creation. As we delve into the Toltec teachings and practices in the chapters that follow, remember that you are embarking on a sacred journey—the journey to reclaim your personal freedom and fully embrace your role as the artist of your life.

Chapter One

A Chorus of Voices

People are often surprised when I tell them that my father and I are huge football fans. When they picture the authors of *The Four Agreements* and *The Mastery of Self* wearing NFL jerseys, eating giant pretzels, and doing the wave, they are either scandalized, disappointed, or delighted, depending on their expectations of what a spiritual author should be. Some of them are afraid that we can't possibly be teaching "real" spirituality if we enjoy such ordinary things. However, people who know my dad well know that he can turn *anything* into a spiritual lesson, and football games are no exception.

Once, we were at a game when I noticed that my father didn't seem to be watching the players in the usual way. Instead, he was sitting back in his chair and seemed to be watching and listening to the entire stadium. I decided to start paying attention in the same way that he was. After a few moments, I noticed that when one team made a good play, half the people in the stadium would cheer, and the other half would boo. And when the other team made a good play, the people who were cheering before would boo, and the people who were booing before would cheer. You could watch the waves of emotion sweeping over the stadium, back and forth, back and forth, like wind blowing in a field.

When he realized what I was doing, my father gave me a knowing smile. "Welcome to the *mitote*," he said.

In the Toltec tradition, we teach that the human mind is filled with thousands of voices all clamoring for our attention. We call this collection of voices the mitote. Some of the voices in our mitote belong to our original caregivers and those who helped raise us: our parents or guardians, teachers, siblings, and extended family. As we get older, we add the voices of our friends, neighbors, classmates, romantic interests, and even professional colleagues. Some of these voices belong to the larger culture: the advertisements, TV shows, movies, newspapers, books, and magazines we absorbed growing up. Over time, these voices take root in our minds; indeed, they can become such a constant and familiar presence that we start to think they are us.

To truly understand the intensity of the mitote, imagine a crowded stadium. If you've ever been to a large sporting event, you know that the sound in the stadium or arena is incredible. Some of these venues can hold up to one hundred thousand fans. Imagine hearing tens of thousands of human voices at once, all competing for your attention—and doing so loudly. Can you feel how loud it is? Can you feel how overwhelming it is?

Now, imagine that every single person in that stadium is expressing an idea, belief, or opinion that you have been offered over the course of your life. Every person is telling you what they think you should do or not do, how you should feel or not feel, what you should value or not value, and, most important, what you should fear or not fear—and each voice is communicating that idea, belief, or opinion in their own way. Some of them are shouting. Some of them are whispering. Some of them are using dynamic props to stir up the drama. In a stadium, they may have their faces painted, wear costumes, or wave big signs. If you think back to the voices that have caught your attention throughout your life, you may find that the most dramatic or memorable ones have also used striking images to get your attention.

Now consider the modern world, the "information age," when the voices of the mitote have more tools than ever before to plant these ideas. Algorithm-driven social media feeds, targeted ads based on what you search for or click on online, and news stories optimized for maximum attention show us a selective view of what is happening around the world. And it all makes its way into our minds, shaping what we want, what we believe, and what we fear. The modern world has supercharged the mitote, and the result is that we live in a time when fear, loneliness, and anxiety are at an all-time high.

As we learn how to deal with the mitote, we will want to understand how the voices of the mitote were created in the first place.

Domestication

In my family's Toltec tradition, we say that virtually all humans go through a process called *domestication*. It works like this: from the moment we're born, we're taught how to behave, what to believe, and how to view the world, all in an effort to assimilate us into society.

Many forms of domestication are helpful and necessary to keep us safe from physical dangers. "Don't touch the hot stove" and "look both ways before crossing the street" are simple examples of necessary forms of domestication. Saying please and thank you, learning to share with others, and telling the truth are other simple forms of domestication that most of us learned as children, and these concepts create the helpful bedrock on which our society functions.

But there are other examples of domestication that aren't as helpful. For example, your parents may teach you, through words or by example, that getting a divorce is the worst thing that can ever happen to you, that you aren't "successful" in life unless you're making a certain amount of money, or that being anything less than physically flawless makes you "less than." So, while a hot stove really can be dangerous, cars really can run kids over, and sharing with others and telling the truth are generally helpful, in other cases the line gets blurred.

Beyond the helpful and necessary domestications, our parents and other caregivers may also domesticate us with their own psychological fears of judgment, failure, scarcity, and shame.

Over time, these negative domestications become the voices in our mitote. If we obey these voices unquestioningly, we go on living our lives according to the standards set by our parents, teachers, and other domesticators, whether or not these standards are true for us. The Toltecs call this phenomenon self-domestication, as now the beliefs of others have become our own primary beliefs, and we ourselves have taken over the job of enforcing them.

Your negative domestications show up in the form of fear-based thoughts such as "you'll never amount to anything," "nobody will ever love you," or even "you'll go to hell." If you dig deeper, you'll likely realize that you've formed agreements based on these domestications—agreements that are standing in the way of living the life you truly desire. Yet all along, these agreements were based on the fears of others: your parents, caregivers, friends, and the society in which you grew up. This chorus of voices—your mitote—is intimidating, and it is powerful, and it may not reflect your true wishes for your life at all!

The Power of Story

Humans are extraordinary creatures. We make tools, create art, express love and tenderness toward one another, and use our intelligence in a myriad of beautiful ways.

We also tell stories.

Perhaps this is our most unique and prolific gift: the ability to create stories in our minds and tell them over and over again, both to others and—most important—to ourselves.

Now consider the impact of the mitote on our story-making ability. When we get shot with a metaphorical poisoned arrow, we can create an entire narrative around the event: "I bet it was my coworker, she's always been jealous of me"; or "I *knew* this would happen someday, nobody's ever really loved me"; or even "I'd better get a good coat of armor so nobody can ever shoot me again." Although we have the capacity to create beautiful stories, a lot of us are more in the habit of creating fearful ones.

The voices in our mitote and the stories they spin arise in countless ways depending on our own individual temperament and unique personality, but they all have one thing in common: they can undermine our ability to be happy, to take action that supports our heart's true desire, and to live our lives to the fullest. They can make us believe that our safety and happiness depend on fulfilling a very strict set of conditions, while blinding us to the full range of possibilities that are available to us. They can convince us that we need to fit into a specific mold to be okay, even when it would be clear to any reasonable outside observer that this isn't true.

In some cases, the stories produced by our mitote can sound so convincing that we don't even recognize them for what they are: the ideas, beliefs, and opinions of others that were planted in us long ago. Instead, we now experience fear-based stories as "facts," not even realizing that there are other ways to think, feel, and be. We may think we're making our own decisions and living our own lives, but if we look deeper, we see that it is fear that is determining everything about the way our lives play out. This revelation itself is terrifying—but it doesn't have to be. It's an opportunity to choose another path. Our options and our actions are not in fact limited; our creativity and optimism are still available to us, and while fear, inertness, and the status quo might currently reign, there is a way forward that's more authentic to who you really are.

Stories and Psychological Fear

The stories in our mitote often run on repeat, continually subjecting us to psychological fear.

Contrast this with wild animals, who live much closer to death than most of us. A caterpillar probably doesn't spend its day wracked with anxiety, thinking, *What if a bird eats me today?* Instead, it goes about its business, eating leaves and looking for a sunny spot to build a cocoon. If and when that caterpillar does get eaten by a bird, its suffering is brief and physical, *not* repeated, prolonged, and psychological.

Human beings, on the other hand, will play and replay imaginary scenarios in our minds, and generate emotions and physical reactions based on these scenarios. Instead of reserving our fear for immediate physical threats, we splash it around freely, using any old excuse to feel afraid.

My younger brother Jose tells a wonderful story about a time our father unexpectedly called him up to speak onstage in front of a packed auditorium—something I experienced with my father as well. Even though Jose was completely safe in a physical sense, his legs turned to jelly, his palms began to sweat, and his mitote began to clamor about how people would judge and laugh at him. As he walked up to the stage, he felt overwhelming psychological fear. Of course, what really happened is that he went up and spoke from his heart, as quietly and calmly as he could. To his surprise, the people in the audience gave him a standing ovation—and he went on to overcome his fear of public speaking.

I had a powerful experience of the mitote's voices leading to psychological fear when my first child was born. The moments after the nurse placed my baby son in my arms for the first time were filled with indescribable bliss. But just seconds later, my mitote began speaking, and that bliss was replaced with fear. *Oh my God, what about sudden infant death syndrome? Babies die from that all the time. I think I read they mostly die in their sleep.* My body flooded with adrenaline as I confronted the possibility of my precious son being struck down by a condition I couldn't control. It was only when I realized that my psychological fear, in the form of worry, was in overdrive that I was able to come back into the present moment and reconnect to the joy and bliss of holding my newborn son.

Two years later, when my son was diagnosed with autism, my mitote went wild. Scary voices in my head started making dire predictions about what his and our family's life would be like as a result of this diagnosis. My son is now in his twenties, and at several points in this book I will share some of the lessons I've learned from our journey, but I want to begin by saying that nothing my mitote said on diagnosis day turned out to be true.

This points to one of the most unhelpful effects of the mitote: worry. Although we may spend the majority of our lives in a state of physical safety, we nevertheless spend much of our time worrying—which is just psychological fear by another name. This is a poor use of our energy and greatly clouds our Personal Dream with negativity. Worry, if not addressed internally, can become a waste of precious time at best and debilitating at worst. Although I use the word *fear* rather than *worry* throughout this book, everything I say about fear applies equally to worry.

Reclaiming Your Yes and No

One of the most important concepts I teach my apprentices is that we all can gain control over our yes and our no. Taking control of your yes means consciously deciding what you're agreeing to, what you're allowing into your life, and where you're giving permission. Taking control of your no means consciously deciding where you're withholding your permission, declining to agree, and setting boundaries.

If you don't recognize the power of your yes and your no and take ownership of it, you can be sure that your mitote will do it for you. Whether it's the voice of an intrusive parent, a controlling partner, or simply the culture at large, someone else's idea or belief will step in to influence your choice, making it seem difficult if not impossible to assert yourself. For example, you may end up "agreeing" that it's too scary to leave the job you're unhappy in, even though you have all the skills and resources you need to do so.

If we aren't aware of it, our yes and our no can be determined by the loudest voice in our mitote. Usually, one voice in our mitote is responsible for generating a fear-based story again and again, reminding us of just how dangerous or unachievable something is, or that we had better go along with something rather than exercising the power of our no. Remember, a story can often be boiled down to a simple phrase, endlessly repeated: for example, *I am not enough* or *There won't be enough*. When our mitote is in charge, our yes and no come from this place rather than our heart's true desire.

Sometimes, you can imagine in vivid detail all the terrible things that might happen when there isn't enough, or when you are not enough. More voices might pipe up in support of the original one, elaborating on its ideas: *There won't be enough, so I can't afford to share . . .* or *I am not enough, and they'll judge me for not being enough, so I won't even try . . .*

As we begin this journey together, the first step is to recognize what your fear-based stories are telling you. By becoming conscious of your specific fears, you can work on confronting them during the moments in which they *aren't* being triggered. In the following exercises, I will share my favorite tools for doing exactly that.

Exercise: Uncover Your Stories

If you haven't yet paused to consider what your own mitote sounds like and the kinds of stories you hear about your own life, set aside a few minutes to do this now. Find a place where you won't be disturbed or interrupted, and consider these prompts: When your mitote gets riled up with fear, what do the loudest voices say? Try writing these stories down as single phrases, such as "I should have finished college," or "I should have taken that job," or "I'm not good with money," or "I'll always be alone."

Although your story may feel unique, chances are that thousands or even millions of people hear similar stories from their own mitotes every day—which should be enough to make you skeptical of the mitote's claims!

Once you've made a list of these phrases, carry it around in your pocket for a week. Every time a voice in your mitote brings up one of these stories, put a checkmark beside it. At the end of the week, which story has the most checkmarks? Are you surprised to see how frequently this story comes up in your day-to-day life? Would you have guessed that this was your dominant fear?

Exercise: Consider Your Commitment

Imagine you get a letter in the mail. This letter contains an official-looking contract. The contract has your name at the top, and a signature field at the bottom, and it states, *In every situation, for the rest of my time on Earth, I agree to act as if_____, whether or not this is factually true.*

Fill in the blank with your top fear from the previous exercise. For example, *In every situation, for the rest of my time on Earth, I agree to act as if I am not enough/ there won't be enough, whether or not this is factually true.*

Next, look at the signature line at the bottom of the contract. Are you going to sign this? What would happen if you didn't agree? Who would you be if you ripped up this contract instead?

Exercise: Write a New Contract

Assuming you said no to the contract in the previous exercise, it's time to write a new contract.

Take out a piece of paper, and write a new agreement for yourself. This new agreement does not have to be the direct opposite of the old one; it can be nuanced. For example, you might write, *I agree to consider the possibility that there might be enough*, or *In the absence of evidence to the contrary, I agree to act as if there is enough.*

How does it feel to communicate your yes in such a clear and intentional way? What happens to the voices in your mitote when you make a conscious decision about your agreements, instead of letting fear dictate your beliefs and actions?

Chapter Two

Fear and Awareness

A couple of times a year, my brother Jose and I take twenty to thirty apprentices on power journeys to the old Toltec city of Teotihuacan, a sacred site near Mexico City that is home to the Pyramids of the Sun and the Moon. Over the course of five days, we visit each plaza and pyramid, inviting our students to examine their fears with unconditional love and release their attachment to stories that are no longer serving them. Not surprisingly, the most common fear apprentices bring to this journey is the fear that they're not enough: not good enough, smart enough, attractive enough, interesting enough, and so on and so forth. Many of these participants are very successful by our modern standards: they often hold advanced degrees, and have high-paying jobs, supportive families, and good health. And yet they too are faced with feelings of insecurity, anxiety, and loneliness.

The fear of not being enough is the most basic psychological fear, and it is perhaps the oldest too. This fear shows up in the cosmology of almost every major religion: from Adam and Eve's casting out from the Garden of Eden to Mara chiding Buddha as he sits under the bodhi tree with the words, "Who do you think you are to walk this path? You are not worthy!" It seems that we have been telling each other this story since the beginning of recorded history.

Often, apprentices sign up for the Teotihuacan power journey when they've had an inkling that an idea, belief, or rule they've been taught doesn't align with their inner truth—yet they're still afraid of what will happen if they let this idea go. They're waiting for someone outside themselves to decide that they are worthy, or to give them proof of their own worth in a way that will conquer this fear forever. Many times, it is only when they reach the very last plaza, on the final day of the trip, that they finally realize that it is not me, not Jose, not their parents, not their partners, but only *they* who can decide that they are worthy. Only they can challenge this domestication and step into a new life.

When it comes to psychological fear, many of us look to the outside for answers. We hope that finding the perfect partner, charming everyone around us, or gaining the approval of a spiritual teacher or guru will make us feel worthy at last, not realizing that we are the only ones who can overcome this fear in a lasting way. By the time they come to Teotihuacan, many apprentices have *already* found wonderful partners, successful careers, and a meaningful spiritual practice, but that root psychological fear still lingers.

Overcoming physical fear often involves exposing yourself to that fear in manageable doses. For example, if you're afraid of swimming in the ocean, you can start by just sitting on the beach, slowly work your way up to standing knee-deep in the waves, then to treading water, and eventually to swimming. By exposing yourself to the feared situation again and again, you slowly learn that the sense of alarm and distress that you feel is out of proportion to the actual risk. You amass a body of evidence showing that, when done in reasonable conditions, with reasonable precautions, swimming in the ocean can be pleasurable and safe.

Overcoming *psychological* fear requires a slightly different approach. This is because, while it is easy to identify the ocean or a snake as a source of fear, it can be hard to recognize all the sneaky ways that a psychological fear has been undermining your personal freedom. For example, perhaps your fear of unworthiness has led you to make a conscious or unconscious agreement with yourself that you will only set "realistic" goals that do not reflect your true potential. While this agreement is rooted in fear, it can easily masquerade as a perfectly responsible and reasonable way to live your life.

Other common examples of how the fear of unworthiness can dominate your life is when you only choose partners to whom you can feel superior—after all, a truly good, honest, and kind partner would only make you feel even more unworthy. Sometimes, this fear manifests in the opposite way, such as when you choose partners who remind you that you aren't worthy, and you feel comfortable in the reinforcement of this belief system, even though it is painful. This is often the case when someone is in a relationship with a person who treats them badly, and everyone else in their life can see it except them.

In both cases, you hold yourself back from reaching for opportunities because you feel that you don't deserve them. Again, you may have done a lot of work to convince yourself that your choices are based in something other than fear, but when you do even a tiny bit of digging, you may find fear at the root.

Often, it's only by reflecting on your life as a whole that you can begin to see patterns and notice how fear-based stories have guided your choices. By building your awareness, you can start to catch these stories *the moment they arise* and begin to reclaim your personal freedom.

Stalking the Mind

The area of Mexico in which the Toltec civilization flourished was home to the jaguar—a huge and fearsome jungle cat revered for its hunting skills as well as its ability to run at speeds of up to fifty miles per hour. Across its range, names for this lean and agile creature translate to phrases like "he who kills with one leap" and "ferocity in battle." To this day, visitors to the forest in rural Mexico are sometimes lucky enough to catch a glimpse of a jaguar—although never before the jaguar sees them first.

The jaguar survives and thrives in the challenging jungle environment thanks to its awareness: the attention it pays to every footfall, every snapping twig, every falling leaf, and every scent wafting on the breeze. It stalks its prey with total focus, yet continues to pay attention to the wider environment. This dual awareness allows it to complete a successful hunt while still monitoring its physical and emotional states and noticing changing factors such as the weather and the presence of other creatures.

In the Toltec tradition, we invoke the wisdom of the jaguar in a process we call "stalking the mind." Just as a jaguar has an exquisite awareness of everything going on in the forest, we too must build our awareness of everything going on in our minds—especially those seemingly automatic processes that feel like "who we are." The prey we hunt are the thoughts, stories, habits, and beliefs that lead us to make the choices we make in life, and all of these are largely the result of our domestication. The harmful domesticated beliefs are the ones we are most interested in, as they are the ones that were put there by the poisoned arrow of fear. The more skilled we get at "catching" this prey, the easier it becomes to free ourselves from fear.

So how can we become masters at stalking our minds? Practice is what makes the master. At a fundamental level, stalking the mind simply refers to the practice of becoming aware of your thoughts, and not believing them to be true without question.

Because this is easier said than done, I've found it helpful to break the process down into four levels of awareness. You can focus on one level at a time, and as you will see, they actually build on each other, strengthening your overall awareness as you go.

Notice Physical Sensations

Building awareness of your mental processes first requires you to become more aware of the sensations in your body. Physical sensations are often the precursors to thought. Sometimes, before a fearful story enters your mind, there may be a sensation in your body first—whether it's a prickle on the back of your neck, a slight increase in your heart rate, or a dampness in your palms.

Often, this response is rooted in past experience, and as a result it can create an emotional and mental trigger. For example, let's say you see someone walking down the street who looks like an ex with whom you had a painful breakup. Before your mind has a chance to tell a story about what's happening, your muscles have tensed, your heart is pounding, and perhaps you've even ducked into a shop or café to avoid that person. Other times, physical responses aren't tied to a past experience but rather to an unquestioned belief or story. For example, you might get a lump in your throat when it's your turn to speak in front of a group because you're afraid that, unlike everyone else who already shared, you have nothing worthwhile to say.

Meditation, a vital practice for stalking the mind, can also help you build awareness. We'll discuss meditation more at the end of this chapter, but in the meantime let's look at some other tools to strengthen physical awareness.

One technique I often recommend is to make a habit of scanning your body at set intervals throughout the day, perhaps at the top of the hour or as close to it as you can. Take a moment to feel your body and answer the following: How's your breathing? What's going on in your gut? Does your chest feel tight and armored, or soft and expansive? What are your hands doing? Do you feel the urge to get a snack, scroll on your phone, or otherwise soothe and distract yourself?

Next, start to look for patterns. Are there certain times of day when you feel more relaxed or tense? Do you express anxiety by wringing your hands or shortening your breath? Which situations trigger these behaviors and sensations in you? Build out from here until you can maintain a subtle but ever-present awareness of your body and its fluctuations throughout the day.

Observe Your Thoughts and Stories

The next step is to build awareness of the connection between thoughts and stories. Sometimes, a thought or story arises directly on the heels of a physical sensation; other times, a thought or story will trigger a physical sensation. Pay attention to what is happening in your mind when you feel that tightness in your chest or dampness in your palms. Does it happen when you think about money? Perhaps you saw a commercial about the importance of "saving for retirement," and it created a sense of anxiety (which is exactly what these commercials are designed to do in most cases). Or perhaps you feel this physical tightness when you contemplate the possibility that your partner will leave you, or when you consider trying something outside your comfort zone, such as applying for a new job or submitting a poem to a writing contest. In other words, begin to notice the specific fears associated with these physical sensations and if there is a trigger that activates them. What are the thoughts and stories behind these fears? (The exercises from chapter 1 can be helpful here.)

Next, start looking for patterns. Are you more prone to having these thoughts when you engage in a certain activity? When the weather is cloudy or cold? When you've just watched the news or read a particularly frightening article online? When you've just gotten off the phone with a specific person?

Also make a habit of noticing the fact that you are thinking. When you find yourself lost in thought, simply speak or think the word "thinking" to call your awareness back to the present moment. Notice the way your mind produces thoughts more or less automatically, the way a plugged-in refrigerator will continue to produce cold air. Start to ask yourself if every one of these thoughts is just as true and important as all the others.

Track Your Emotions

Once you've had some practice observing your thoughts and stories, it's time to raise your awareness of the emotions that arise from them, paying particular attention to fear, anxiety, dread, and worry.

The goal here is to realize that it's often the thoughts and stories we believe to be true that produce the emotions we experience. In other words, when it comes to psychological fear, the truth is that most of the time we're scaring ourselves. For example, if your partner doesn't text you back right away, you may not notice or mind—but if you have a story that your partner doesn't care, is hiding things from you, or is in danger in some way, you may feel anger, worry, or even dread. These emotions aren't provoked by anything real that happened in the world, but simply by your stories and predictions about what might be happening.

Some of you reading this might be saying to yourself, *Wait, my story really is true! I have a reason to be fearful.* We will continue to look at this in the next chapter, but for now I'd like to ask you to be open to the possibility that the scary stories you tell yourself aren't true. And yes, I really do mean all of them.

Become a Watcher

In this last step, I invite you to zoom out to a place where you can observe the activity of your mind, body, and emotions all at once. Imagine yourself floating above your physical body and watching everything that's going on from a small distance, the same way you would sit by the ocean and watch the waves. Ask yourself who is doing the noticing here. Are "you" the thoughts and sensations? Or are you the one who's watching them from a distance?

This silent awareness has many names, such as the observer, the watcher, the nagual, consciousness, or the field in which everything occurs. The name you give it is not important; what matters is that at this level of awareness, you are distancing yourself, and as a result you are not fully wrapped up in your thoughts and stories, emotions, and physical sensations. This level of awareness can be hard to maintain when you're in the midst of a crisis, but if you practice on a consistent basis, you'll find that you can stay calm and detached even in challenging and chaotic circumstances. More often than not, if you observe your current state in this way, the crisis will change too.

By practicing at this level of awareness, you will begin to understand the complex interplay between your inner consciousness and your outer world—in other words, you will see just how much your mitote and domestication have filtered your experience of life. How does your Personal Dream affect your interactions with other people, your decision to take risks or not, and your assessment of real or imaginary threats? In what ways are these aspects of your Personal Dream helping and supporting you? In what ways are they holding you back? What would it be like to change them?

Putting It Together

Each level of awareness builds on the previous ones, and all are invaluable when it comes to facing the poison of fear. Developing a keen awareness of your physical sensations makes it easier to catch fearful thoughts as they arise. Catching fearful thoughts helps you understand the narratives that trigger the emotions you experience and that shape your Personal Dream. Carefully observing the ways your Personal Dream is creating your life provides the opportunity for you to choose another way.

Developing the awareness of a jaguar doesn't happen overnight—but once this awareness is established and maintained, you will begin to experience more peace in your life. There is something about just having the awareness of what's happening that allows us to choose differently. The important thing is to practice this awareness consistently, and to recommit to the practice when you inevitably get sidetracked. This is how you will catch the machinations of fear, which can be very subtle, before fear has a chance to take over your actions. When you become aware, all the unconscious fear and beliefs that have been dictating your actions are brought into the light—and you finally have the opportunity to choose differently.

A friend of mine began stalking her mind and realized that she had the most fearful thoughts and stories on Mondays, even though she loved her job and looked forward to doing it. Puzzled by this discovery, she decided to back up and focus on her physical sensations. After a few weeks, she realized that on Mondays her muscles ached after spending all weekend hiking, gardening, and doing projects around the house. Her anxious thoughts were a response to the pain in her body and had nothing to do with her work. She also noticed how she had bought into the common societal notion about the "Monday blues," which refers to the dread of starting a work week, especially for those who dislike their jobs. The combination of these revelations helped her put her thoughts in context, refrain from acting on her fears, and take steps to alleviate the physical suffering giving rise to them in the first place.

Another friend realized that whenever he spoke to his mother on the phone, his negative stories became more prominent for the next twenty-four hours. Not only that, but he would become more identified with those stories, temporarily losing his ability to see them for the filters on reality they really were. In response to this discovery, he decided that he would not make any important decisions in the twenty-four-hour period immediately following a phone call with his mother. This policy saved him from taking unnecessary and harmful actions out of a temporarily increased sense of fear. Over time, the very act of noticing this pattern lessened the fear and negative stories in his mind. He also had a more charitable mindset when talking with his mother; instead of dreading their conversations, he realized that she was scaring herself with her domestication—but he was no longer scared.

Like my friends, you will know that you are mastering the practice of stalking your mind when you begin to have different responses to the presence of fear as it makes itself known in your body and mind. A physical sensation that used to provoke a fear spiral will no longer do so; a mental story that used to launch you into immediate and unquestioned action will simply be one perspective among several you are considering. Instead of letting the poison on the arrow make your decisions for you, you will reclaim your agency, choosing how to shape your Personal Dream based on love and wisdom instead of fear.

As you become a master hunter, you will even find that in some cases you can perceive the poisoned arrow coming from a mile away, and avoid it altogether. Like the jaguar who hears a snapping twig from a hundred feet away, you can hear that arrow whistling toward you and say, "Not today."

This doesn't mean controlling every aspect of life so you are never hurt or uncertain—that is, after all, impossible. We all must live with uncertainty and change. Rather, by applying the antidote of awareness and curiosity, you diffuse the power of fear almost instantly. Okay, so you may not know what will happen—but isn't there something wonderful in that too? Danger need not lurk around every corner. There are also opportunities for surprise, happy encounters, new discoveries. We cannot have all the facts about our circumstances and our surroundings; but we can approach our world as though the stories we tell ourselves are just as important as knowing everything. With this shift in perspective, soon you'll find that fear doesn't have a chance to enter your consciousness at all.

The exercises that follow are all designed to help you become highly skilled at stalking your own mind. We will be using this skill throughout the rest of the book, so please take your time and return to these often.

Exercise: The Link Between Sensations and Stories

Mental stories are often preceded by physical sensations, and often they are so subtle or fleeting we don't even notice them. In this exercise, I invite you to build your awareness of the link between your body and mind.

First, think of a part of your body that gives you trouble, such that you can't help but be aware of it on a regular basis: an aching back, a sore knee, a recurring headache. For the next week, take note of the time and place when you notice this part hurting, as well as the thoughts and stories running through your mind when it is there.

Ask yourself which came first: the physical pain or the stories. Do these stories appear at any other time, or only when you are in physical pain? What do you think would happen to these stories if this physical pain was cured? Would they still exist? How much of the story is "true," and how much is just your mind's attempt to explain the pain?

Exercise: Shoulds and Woulds

Fear manifests in our minds in gross and subtle ways: both as loud and detailed horror movies and as quiet but persistent inner scoldings. As you practice stalking your mind, pay careful attention to *shoulds* and *woulds*, as fear-based beliefs and stories often burrow within these seemingly innocuous phrases. Do you tell yourself things like *I should really take down that post I wrote before anyone reads it* or *If I was really a good parent, I would have noticed my daughter's illness earlier*? Thoughts like these point the way to deep fears, which we are sometimes scarcely conscious of.

The next time you have a thought involving a should or a would, pause and notice. Out loud or in your head, ask the fear behind this thought to show itself to you. Are you afraid of being exposed as flawed, ridiculous, or unworthy? Are you afraid of losing someone's love, including your own?

Imagine you are holding this fear in front of you, where you can get a good look at it. Take your time. Fears thrive in secrecy; the more comfortable you get with taking them out and examining them, the faster they shrink. See how fast you can get at catching your shoulds and woulds before they slip by unnoticed.

Exercise: Stalking the Mind Meditation

For this meditation, you will want to be in a comfortable place where you can sit or lie down without being disturbed for twenty to thirty minutes.

Close your eyes and breathe normally. Bring your attention to the present moment by focusing on your body, paying close attention to any pain and tension, as well as to areas of comfort and relaxation. I recommend starting from either the top of your head or from your toes, and move slowly all the way up or down your body, paying attention to how each area feels as you do so.

After you've completed a scan of your body, keep your focus on the present moment. It can be helpful to simply notice that you are breathing. We take thousands of breaths each day, few of which we notice, and yet the breath is often the connection between the body and the mind.

As you focus on the present moment and watch your breath, notice the thoughts, stories, and emotions that arise as you do so. For the next several minutes, simply notice the thoughts and narratives that come to your mind and any emotions they produce. Do any of these feel especially urgent? When you catch yourself going down a thought chain, simply return to your breath and remember you are in the present moment. Do not chide or beat yourself up for these thoughts; simply let them go and see what else arises.

For the last few minutes of your meditation, imagine that you have an eagle-eye view of your mind and body. You are above your physical sensations, your thoughts, your stories, and your emotions. Notice that they are not you.

When you are ready, bring your awareness back into your body. Wiggle your fingers and toes, and if you moved into a lying-down position during meditation, slowly sit up. Take a moment to stretch and reacclimate to the room and your body.

Once your meditation is complete, make a mental list of what thoughts, stories, and emotions arose for you. Were you replaying things that have happened in the past? Were you thinking ahead to your to-do list for later that day? The thoughts and stories that arise when we are meditating can often show us the areas in our lives where we have the most fear. Simply knowing that you have extra fear around a certain area in your life can help you gently create more space between your thoughts and the actions you take. For example, you cannot change what happened in the past, but you can move forward with more intention, knowing that you're doing your best—and it's likely that most everyone else is, too. If you've set yourself up for failure with a too-long to-do list, you can address those feelings of anxiety and time scarcity by prioritizing your tasks and determining what must be done versus what can wait until tomorrow or next week. Meditation isn't the time to work through your thoughts, stories, and emotions, but it can shine a light on what is troubling you. From there, you know what to focus on once your meditation has concluded.

Chapter Three

The Dreaming Mind

It's said that after Siddhārtha Gautama attained enlightenment under the bodhi tree, people could tell that something about him had changed, but they couldn't quite put their finger on what. When they asked him what had happened, he simply replied, "I am now awake." In the Pali language, the root word *budh-* means "to awaken," which is how the Buddha got his title and the tradition received its name. By waking up to eternal truths about life, death, and suffering, the Buddha could never again fall for the same old illusions that normally dominate a human life.

The Hindu tradition likewise emphasizes the dreamlike nature of our everyday lives, and our tendency to get caught up in *maya*, or illusion. In a popular story, Narada, a wandering saint, asks Lord Krishna to explain the concept of maya. Krishna agrees, but he asks Narada to bring him a glass of water first, as he is very thirsty. When Narada knocks on the door of a nearby hut to ask for some water, a beautiful young woman answers. Before Narada knows it, he's become swept up in a dream: he marries the woman, has children and grandchildren, and forgets all about his quest to understand the nature of illusion. It's only when a devastating flood sweeps away his family that he calls out to Krishna in despair, and realizes he's been living in maya all along.

In the Toltec tradition, we also say that the human mind is dreaming all the time, and if we aren't aware of our mind's habit of dreaming, it means that in an important way we are asleep—even when we are physically awake! Just like the Buddha under the bodhi tree or Narada in the flood, we want to awaken from these dreams and rid ourselves of the unnecessary fear and suffering they provoke.

Every one of us has a Personal Dream—a filter through which we screen the raw experiences of reality. This filter is made up of our own past experiences and related projections, speculations, fears, and biases. Of course, our Personal Dream is also colored by our domestications, our desires, our values, and our beliefs. No matter where we go or what we do, we will see life through the lens of our Personal Dream, and this has a profound effect on how we experience our day-to-day life.

To illustrate this better, let's look at how two people can derive entirely different meanings from the same event. For example, one person could find a hundred-dollar bill on the sidewalk and think, *Wow! The universe is smiling on me today. This is a sign I'm meant to buy something nice.* A different person could come across that same hundred-dollar bill and think, *There's no way I'm going to pick that up. What if someone thinks I stole it? What if this is a test and I'm on camera, and people are watching to see what I do?*

For the first person, their Personal Dream is causing them to see blessings, good luck, and abundance when they look at the hundred-dollar bill. For the second person, their Personal Dream is such that when they see the hundred-dollar bill, they have fears about being tested, judged, and possibly even punished for picking it up. Neither of these responses is right or wrong, but both are rooted in the Personal Dream of the individual. The key point is that both people respond to the hundred-dollar bill by making up a *story* about what it means, why it's there, and what will happen if they take it.

When you take every human's Personal Dream and put them all together, you get what we call the Dream of the Planet: the ever-shifting, ever-evolving set of beliefs, ideals, and stories formed by our collective agreements.

To see the Personal Dream and the Dream of the Planet in action, consider all the levels of dreaming that go into the hundred-dollar bill example. First of all, when you spot a hundred-dollar bill, all you're *really* seeing is a piece of paper with ink on it. It is only in our current Dream of the Planet that this particular type of paper and ink has value that other plant material doesn't have—if you could time-travel to the Middle Ages and go on a shopping spree, you'd soon realize that your windfall was worthless, because the Dream of the Planet at that time didn't recognize paper money.

Next, let's take a closer look at your potential reaction to finding the money. If you worry that someone will think you stole it, that's because the current Dream of the Planet contains ideas about ownership and personal property, as well as ideas about the importance of other people's opinions. On the other hand, if you think it's your lucky day and the universe is smiling on you, that's because the Dream of the Planet *also* contains concepts like luck, synchronicity, and divine benevolence.

The Dream of the Planet has looked very different through different eras of human history. For example, in past eras, the Dream of the Planet included pantheons of gods and goddesses who had to be worshipped and whose favor had to be carefully courted in order to avoid starvation and disease; people feared incurring the wrath of these gods. In the current Dream of the Planet, we are less likely to fear the wrath of gods, and more likely to fear acts of terrorism and war, natural disasters such as hurricanes, earthquakes, and fires, or hackers who can bring down the electronic systems that we all rely on.

Every Personal Dream goes into the Dream of the Planet, but the Dream of the Planet also plays an important part in coloring our Personal Dreams. For example, if all the people around you are very concerned about social status, you are more likely to have a Personal Dream that includes the fear of losing face. And if you grow up in a society that values material wealth, you are more likely to carry this value into your own Personal Dream—at least, until you wake up from the dream and begin to make conscious decisions about which stories you wish to tell.

Dreaming and the Word

Those of you familiar with Toltec teachings already know that in our tradition, we place great importance on how we use our word. Indeed, the first agreement in my father's bestselling book *The Four Agreements* is *be impeccable with your word*. I know many of you have read that book, and I encourage you to do so if you haven't. As my father points out, language has allowed us to share ideas, build bodies of knowledge, pass down information from generation to generation, and create the elaborate civilizations we know today.

Something you may not have realized, though, even if you have read *The Four Agreements*, is that words are both the primary filter for our Personal Dream and the foundation for how we cocreate the

Dream of the Planet. Our relationship with words is closely tied to our relationship with both dreams. Just as many aspects of the Dream of the Planet were forged through millions of agreements made with words, our Personal Dream is likewise shaped by the words that make up our own internal agreements.

So, while language is our most powerful tool for creation, it is also the most common way we get lost in the dream. We can get so caught up in words that we forget they only have power because we agree with their meanings. As Alan Watts famously said, "The menu is not the meal." In other words, although words allow us to communicate with one another, they in and of themselves have no power until we collectively imbue them with meaning.

As children, words were the primary instrument of our domestication. We heard things like "Don't touch that!" and "Pick that up right away," which signaled to us that we were brushing too close to something dangerous or breaking a taboo. In some cases, we also heard things like, "Why can't you be more like your brother?" or "Are you stupid? Don't do it like that." At the time, these words were probably very hurtful. However, if you take a step back, you can see that it wasn't the literal sounds coming out of the mouths of our domesticators that harmed us; it was the fact that we believed them to be true. We gave them power by our agreement—and we can withdraw that power once we become aware.

Words are tools of the dream. They have no independent existence; you can't touch them or hold them in your hand, and they can't in themselves hurt you. Therefore, if the words somebody says cause you to feel fear, that fear is by definition psychological.

Our stalking-the-mind practice can help us see the dreamlike characteristics of words and allow us to detach from them enough that we don't automatically agree with them—especially when it comes to words that create fear. This is much easier said than done, but by recognizing words for what they are—tools of the dream builder—we can begin to release any negative power they have over us.

The Comparison Trap

Another common way we get trapped in the Dream of the Planet is when we compare ourselves to others, typically in the arena of accomplishments, appearance, and life path. Comparing ourselves to others is so common and automatic that we often don't even realize that we're doing it, but it can be a tremendous source of fear. This is another area where our stalking-the-mind practice can be a big benefit to us.

Think about all the ways you compare yourself to others when you meet them for the first time. Do you notice their appearance first, comparing their level of attractiveness, fitness, and apparent health to yours? Do you do this with everyone you meet, or are your comparisons more intense when you meet someone of the same age and gender who runs in the same social circles as you? What about material possessions—the clothes or jewelry the other person is wearing or the car they drive?

Perhaps you also compare yourself to other people's career achievements or social status, feeling either envy or superiority depending on your assessment of where everybody falls. Maybe you even include considerations such as how far along you think they are on the spiritual path, thinking something like, *Well they may have more money than me, but I'm clearly more enlightened than they are.*

When you notice your comparisons, you are also more likely to notice the fear that arises as a result of them in the form of insidious thoughts such as *I'll never be as pretty as her / as wealthy as him / as enlightened as that guy*, and on and on and on. The comparison game is a losing one, and not just because there will always be a world in which you are at some point "inferior." The problem is that determining your own superiority solely through others' perceived lowliness leaves you constantly attacking others in service of defending your superiority—and if your life is spent defending your superiority, you will find yourself with little space to grow or learn. Comparing can only lead to more fear, and it ensures that your true life force, the nagual, remains obscured.

This brings up another important point. While it's vital to learn the practice of stalking the mind, there is no need to beat yourself up when you realize that you've been caught by a dream. The comparison habit is not a personal problem, but simply the way the mind has been conditioned to work in the current Dream of the Planet, which emphasizes personal accomplishment. From a very young age, we are told that if we just do the right things, we too can become rich, successful, and beautiful—and if for some reason things don't work out, we have only ourselves to blame.

Getting caught up in comparisons means getting caught up in a dream—and when you wake up, those comparisons will feel very strange and silly indeed. You may even struggle to remember what made them feel so important at the time. From this waking state, you no longer see comparisons, but only the nagual expressing itself in an infinite number of ways—a dance you can enjoy instead of fearing.

Exercise: Remembering You Are Dreaming

Fear will have a much harder time infiltrating your Personal Dream if you are conscious about the fact that you are dreaming—in other words, if you are aware of your mind's tendency to create stories.

Throughout the day, make a habit of silently repeating the words *I am dreaming*.

As you do so, take a breath and look around. Imagine you are seeing the world through new eyes, uncolored by your habitual stories and unencumbered by past traumas. Who would you be if you had no past? Who would you be if you had no fixed ideas about good or bad or the way things are "supposed" to be?

Notice if your fearful stories have a harder time taking control when you remember that you are dreaming, as opposed to when you are asleep. Can you maintain this awareness for longer and longer periods of time throughout your day? Can you get to a point where you rarely forget you are dreaming at all?

Exercise: Thoughts Versus Facts

Many times, fear makes us forget that we are dreaming—and before we know it, we're reacting to imaginary stories instead of reality, and nothing anybody can say can make us wake up. In this exercise, I invite you to build your awareness that you are dreaming, no matter how intense that dream may be.

The next time you find yourself triggered by fear, worry, or uncertainty, with your mind generating story after story about what might happen, pause and take out a piece of paper.

Draw a line down the middle of the page. On one side of the line, write down the word *Thoughts*. On the other side, write down the word *Facts*.

For example, let's say you've been having a rough time in your relationship and your partner goes on a camping trip with his friends. Under the *Thoughts* column, jot down all the fantasies, speculations, and stories your Personal Dream is trying to impose on the truth. Be as specific as you can. Perhaps it would look like this: *My partner wishes he was with someone more fun and less serious than me, and he's spending the whole camping trip with his friends asking them for their advice on how to break up with me.* Later on, it will be useful to have a record of *exactly* which story your dream was feeding you.

Under the *Facts* column, write down the bare facts of the situation. For example, *My partner is on a camping trip with his friends, I won't hear from him for a few days, and I'm feeling anxious.*

It can be helpful to see what are the facts and what are the stories, assumptions, and fantasies you have created. Seeing it on paper in front of you allows you to stay focused on just the facts.

Repeat this exercise anytime you feel anxious or worried over a situation. Saving these pages can be helpful for the next exercise.

Exercise: Reviewing Old Stories

Once you've completed the previous exercise several times, go back and look at your lists.

Now that the events in question have passed, can you see any patterns in your stories and the accompanying fears that arise in your Personal Dream? For example, if you continue to have stories about your relationship, it may suggest that you have an underlying fear of abandonment. Or if you have many anxious moments related to finances, it may point to a fear of scarcity, or a lack of trust in your own ability to meet your needs.

Becoming aware of your recurring fears can help you identify unhelpful beliefs you might have, and inspire you to act and chart a new course that's not tied to these entrenched habits and beliefs.

Chapter Four

Happiness and Desire

Have you ever had the experience of standing in line to buy or sign up for something you really wanted, only to realize that that thing may run out before you get to the front? As the line inches forward, you start to obsess over whether or not you're going to get it. You start to feel a sense of urgency that quickly spills over into fear. What started out as a simple desire for an ice cream cone or a seat on a plane quickly turns into a form of intense mental suffering. Your mind may even begin to conjure stories of how unhappy you will be if you don't get the thing you're waiting for.

Chances are you've experienced how easily the desire for something can shift into the fear of not getting it. You think about how disappointed you'll be if you don't get your wish, and this makes your desire seem all the more urgent. Yet when you do get what you want, the pleasure you experience doesn't last for nearly as long as you expected; in some cases, you spend more time fearing you'll miss out than you do enjoying the thing itself!

With all this as context, it might be tempting to say that all desire is a bad thing, and it must be eliminated in order to overcome fear. Yet in Toltec cosmology, we see desire as a useful and productive creative force—when we relate to it appropriately. Indeed, we believe it was the desire of the nagual to experience all the different flavors and colors of life that created the whole world. In other words, the life force is desire: the desire to taste, touch, see, hear, experience, and manifest in myriad forms.

Many spiritual traditions tell some version of the following story about the nagual: At the beginning of time, God created the universe. But since the universe and everything in it was God, it meant there was nobody for God to play with except herself. To deal with this vexing situation, God decided to invent a game in which she forgot who she was. By forgetting who she was, God could hide herself in all kinds of people, animals, and things, and enjoy all of our dramas and adventures without getting bored. Every now and then, one of those people would wake up and remember she was God, and after a joyful reunion, the game could start all over again.

I love the image of God (or the creator, or coyote, or whatever you call it) hiding herself in a fern, a star, a human, and everything in between, just waiting to be found. This exuberant desire to exist permeates the entire universe. Without this desire, fish wouldn't swim and trees wouldn't leaf, and human beings wouldn't bother to sing, paint, build, procreate, eat, or undertake the thousands of other actions that make up a life. The desire for beauty, love, meaning, and adventure can inspire us to do great things—it can even inspire us to discover our own divine nature in the form of the nagual. In its most positive sense, desire literally makes the world go round.

Sometimes desire gets mixed up when we become attached to the results or object of that desire. Instead of enjoying the process of painting, we worry about whether our work will be good enough to hang in a gallery or sell at a show. Instead of relishing the experience of falling in love with a new person, we start to wonder if that person will stay with us forever, if they will disappoint us in some way, or if they will even abandon us. Instead of allowing desire to be a creative force in our lives, and remaining open and curious to where it leads, we try to push it in a certain direction. We pile on our fears and insecurities until desire ceases to be a creative force and becomes a tool of control. Instead of enjoying the cosmic game of hide-and-seek, we cross our arms and refuse to play—until some thread of love or magic draws us in again.

Letting Go of Attachments

In the Toltec tradition, we say that when you become attached to the results of your desire, you have put conditions on your happiness. You start saying, *I need this to happen for me to be happy,* or *I need this person to love me so I can feel complete*, instead of allowing desire to follow its natural flow. We do this because deep down we're afraid that we need this object or accomplishment in order to be complete. By attaching ourselves to results and outcomes, we try to shore up our ego and temporarily alleviate those fears. We've forgotten that we are already complete, regardless of what happens with our desires.

Many of us complain about being stuck in careers or life situations that don't match our desires—yet meanwhile we are afraid to try something new. We're attached to our social status, financial security, or sense of identity and don't want to risk making a change. We have a deep fear of losing what we have, even though we don't really want it anymore. We want to move toward our desire, but only if we are guaranteed to get the same status and security we enjoyed before. By inserting this "only if" clause, the ego cleverly maintains control, turning true desire into demands and attachments.

Often it is our domestication that makes it very difficult to tell the difference between healthy desires, which have no attachment to outcomes, and unhealthy demands, which do. From a young age, we are bombarded with advertisements telling us that if we buy the right things, consume the right products, attend the right educational programs, and get into the right careers, we can be assured of happiness and success. Our culture loves to push the acquisition of goods and status as the ultimate goal, and so many of us choose this over our personal freedom. As a consequence, we get attached to results, instead of enjoying the process of exploration and seeing where it leads. Not only that, but we learn to fear that if we don't get these results, we will never be happy.

For example, consider the experience of getting a new car (or a new-to-you car). On the day you received the car, you probably felt great—maybe even blissful. But what happened after a few weeks or months? Suddenly, the new car didn't do it for you like it used to do. In the Toltec tradition we would say that it isn't the car that made you happy. Your happiness was in the temporary cessation of the desire, not the car itself. If it were the car making you happy, it would continue to do that for you, day after day and year after year.

The fact that happiness stems from the temporary cessation of desire, as opposed to some object or milestone, is actually a good thing, because it points to the fact that the happiness is inside you, not outside of you in the world. It's like my grandmother always said: any time we put our faith in something outside of ourselves, we are setting ourselves up for fear, because things in the world are constantly changing and collapsing.

In the current Dream of the Planet, most human minds are trained to chase an end point: we think there will be a moment when we will finally be happy, safe, content, or fulfilled. We tell ourselves, *I'll be satisfied when I get this, or accomplish that*. But even when we reach those goals, they never do the trick for long. Instead, we soon find that our lives feel just as uncertain as before.

This is the desire dilemma. We are never satisfied for very long. Our goal, then, is to remember that it's okay to desire things while trying to not become attached to getting them—to remember that they do not, they cannot, complete us. If we experience fear that our desire won't be fulfilled, it means we have become attached to it.

As you begin to examine your desire, remember that nothing is gained by lying to yourself, saying "I don't really want that," when in fact you do. Rather, working with desire is an invitation to be honest with yourself and accept that you want something, while reminding yourself that achieving the object of your desire won't make you happy in a lasting way. The goal is to cultivate the ability to engage with a desire in a moment of time, remembering that it is finite, and enjoy the moment without the fear of loss. This is how we can engage with desire without becoming unhealthily attached.

Selfish and Unselfish Desires

Another way of evaluating your desires is by asking yourself the question: Is it selfish or not? This is a lost art in the modern world, where the message from society is often based on scarcity and competition. In the current Dream of the Planet, you may have been domesticated to go get what you want before someone else does, or to grasp for wealth and opportunities without considering the impact this has on others or on the planet.

To be clear, personal desires aren't inherently bad. Most of the time, the things we want are reasonable: good food to eat, fulfilling work, happy relationships. Still, it's good to periodically pause and ask ourselves whether fulfilling our desire is coming at the expense of someone else or the community as a whole, and curb our impulses accordingly if necessary.

A simple example of how we curb our personal desires for the social good is by respecting handicapped parking spaces, which are always located near the entrance of a business. Most of us recognize that a person on crutches or using a wheelchair needs the "good" parking more than the rest of us, and are therefore willing to park at the very back of the lot rather than park in a spot needed by someone with mobility issues. In most cases, it's not the threat of a fine that prevents us from grabbing the handicapped spot, but our sense of right and wrong. We know that the convenience that comes from fulfilling our desire isn't worth the hardship it would cause to someone else.

In some cases, we work hard to disguise our selfish desires from ourselves. We say, "Sure, I'm buying a bigger house than I really need, but when my brother and his kids come to visit at Christmas they'll enjoy the extra room. It's really for them, not for me." When this happens, we can take a step back and ask ourselves if fulfilling this desire is truly necessary for a happy and healthy life, or if we could make a choice that benefits an even greater number of beings.

Desire Without Fear

There is a common misconception that spiritual teachers and so-called "enlightened" masters have rid themselves of all desire. Catholic priests don't marry; some Buddhist monks don't eat meat or drink alcohol; Hindu ascetics may give up basic comforts like shoes or even clothing. One might assume that, having transcended all personal desires, they enjoy lives of blissful simplicity devoted to serving others and worshiping God. While this may be true in some cases, it's more often the case that, far from being *free* of desires, they are simply no longer controlled or defined by them. In other words, they have reached a stage where they can feel desire, *but they understand that the fulfillment of that desire will not complete them.*

This realization may seem like an unobtainable spiritual goal to some of you reading this, but I bet you have experienced this in your life already, as the following example shows.

Remember when you were a child, and you really wanted a new toy—perhaps a G.I. Joe doll, a Barbie, or a new video game? At one point in your life, you wanted that toy so badly it kept you up at night, and you probably felt thrilled if you did in fact receive it—whereas not getting it likely resulted in a huge disappointment. But if I were to offer you that same toy now, you would probably decline it without hesitation. Not getting that toy would not create a fear inside you, because you now view the toy as unimportant or unnecessary for your happiness. Growth and change have taken place inside of you, and you genuinely know that having this toy now is not necessary for your happiness.

Now, contrast how you feel about me offering you a toy to if I were to offer you a long weekend in the Bahamas, or some other item, goal, or experience that is tempting to you as an adult. Chances are you would feel a surge of desire to have it—but I can assure you that the excitement after you acquire or experience this thing wouldn't satisfy you for long. A quick look at the lives of the richest people on the planet easily confirms this: they seem to be constantly acquiring luxury goods, buying and selling mega mansions, and jetting off to exotic destinations.

The day you can view your desires with the indifference with which you do the childhood toy, you'll know you have reached the end of all fear. It means that you know in your deepest core what

Jesus, Buddha, Krishna, and a host of other spiritual masters from other traditions have discovered: you are the nagual and the nagual is you. There is nothing you need to possess in order to complete yourself, because you are already complete in this moment. To be clear, this doesn't mean you no longer experience desire; it just means that you are equally happy if you don't get something as when you do.

One of my favorite quotes from the sacred Hindu text the Bhagavad Gita is "Detachment doesn't mean that you own nothing; it means that nothing owns you." To me, this quote deeply relates to living in the present moment. We are owned by our desires to the extent that we are attached to the past—whether that's a past identity, time or money we've invested, or status we've accrued—or the future, placing conditions on what we think we must have in order to be happy. When we come fully into the present, that ownership dissolves, and the world becomes brand-new.

Imagine if you could want something very deeply, yet feel absolutely no fear or anxiety about whether or not you would get it. Imagine if you could possess something priceless, yet feel absolutely no fear or anxiety that you would someday lose it. In the Toltec tradition, we say that you already possess this priceless gift, the nagual energy within, and there is no way you can lose it, for it is synonymous with you. Fear, by definition, occurs when we lose sight of this truth and let our awareness of it become covered up by identification with the *tonal*, or physical matter. Putting our focus on the tonal is the biggest domestication of all.

Remembering that we are the nagual is what aligns us with pure desire—the endlessly creative, productive desire of the nagual manifesting the universe into being. Pure desire exists in the present moment, independent of an imaginary past or future. Pure desire doesn't attach to outcomes; it simply creates, like a vine naturally drawn toward the sun.

Happiness and Desire

Most of us don't experience desire in this way. Instead, we feel obsession or desire attached to a particular outcome. We have tied our inner peace to the fulfillment of some desire, and can't accept not having the thing we crave, whether that's a material object, the approval of others, or the attainment of a goal. We think that having the outcome we want will make our lives inherently better or more worthwhile than some different outcome, and forget that the nagual, or life force, is present in all situations, in all outcomes. Instead of loving ourselves and life unconditionally, we tell ourselves we will love life only if we get our way.

Experiencing desire without fear is one and the same as loving life unconditionally. And loving life unconditionally is the secret that yogis, monks, and wisdom keepers from all traditions have taught for thousands of years.

Exercise: Releasing Fear

Often, we are not conscious of the shadow side of fear lurking beneath our desires. In this exercise, I invite you to uncover the hidden conditions you're attaching to your desires—then release them for good.

First, make a list of your most intense desires. This might include things like acquiring financial security or social status, having children, a certain career, or going on a big adventure. Next, ask yourself if there is any dread or anxiety attached to these desires. What are you afraid will happen if you don't get what you want?

Now think of a time in your life *before* you had this desire, even if that means going back to early childhood. Remember that you once experienced happiness and fulfillment before it even occurred to you to want this thing. You have just proved to yourself that you are capable of being happy and fulfilled, even without having the thing you now want.

Whenever you feel anxiety or dread about not getting your desire, consciously remember how happy you have been in the past, before you ever wanted this thing. By working with this practice consistently, you can learn to feel desire without fear.

Exercise: Foregoing Your Desires

Many of us are whipped around by our desires, constantly pursuing things we want without pausing to consider whether they truly make us happy. Throughout the day, desires for food, sex, distraction, and entertainment are constantly arising, and we often respond to those desires automatically, moving to satisfy them as quickly as we can.

The next time you are in a position to get something you really want, I encourage you to decline it just for the sake of breaking the habit. For example, if you normally say yes to dessert after Sunday dinner, say no. If you normally relax on the couch with a TV series after work, clean the kitchen instead.

Notice that you don't die when you don't fulfill your every desire.

By working with this practice regularly, you take back your power and begin to eliminate the fear associated with not getting what you want.

Exercise: Appreciating What You Didn't Choose

Sometimes, we end up in a situation which is the *opposite* of what we said we wanted—only to discover that it's even better than what we originally desired. In this exercise, I invite you to make a habit of reflecting on all the times you didn't get what you wanted, and celebrating that fact.

First, call to mind a situation in life that you originally resisted, but that turned out well in the end—for example, moving to a new town or taking a job that fell outside your planned career goals. Next, allow yourself to become aware of all the wonderful things that came into your life as a result of this "unwanted" change: new friends, interesting hobbies, a meaningful life path. Allow yourself to feel awe, wonder, and reverence at the mysterious ways the nagual worked through you to bring you where you are today. Can you live with greater trust in life now that you've already seen that getting what you didn't want can turn out so nicely?

Chapter Five

Unconditional Love and Acceptance

The word *love* is one of the most powerful *and* one of the most overused words in the English language. On the one hand, saying the words "I love you" can be the most courageous act of a lifetime. But we also use the word *love* to talk about our favorite restaurants, TV shows, and flavors of ice cream.

With the word *love* being used to signify everything from the most important feelings and experiences in our lives to some of the most ephemeral ones, an alien visiting from another planet would be hard-pressed to identify exactly what this love thing means. Most likely, that alien would conclude that the word *love* is synonymous with enjoyment—enjoyment of a relationship, place, experience, situation, or thing.

Yet as any earthling knows, love is more complicated than mere enjoyment. After all, we don't stop loving our kids on days when the laundry is piling up, the trash needs taking out, and we barely have five minutes for ourselves. We don't stop loving our dogs and cats when they eat our shoes or throw up on the carpet. Whether it's a marriage, a friendship, or a relationship with a sibling, any long and meaningful connection is going to include tough moments that neither person enjoys very much, yet the love endures.

In its deepest form, love is an emotional and spiritual bond which transcends mere pleasure and enjoyment. Indeed, love gives us the strength to do things that are anything but pleasant, such as making painful sacrifices so that our children or partner can have what they need to thrive, or showing up for a friend even when they're not very nice to be around. It is our love for a person that makes us miss them when they go away, worry about them when they're sick, and mourn them when they die. In this sense, love is inextricably bound up with emotions like sorrow and grief, as well as with states like anxiety, jealousy, and fear.

The Opposite of Fear

It's often said that the opposite of fear is love, and in many ways this is true. Yet loving another person can also trigger our deepest fears of being hurt or abandoned, and our relationships with the people we love can become a tremendous source of suffering as a result. The intoxicating feeling of falling in love with someone can be followed by the fear of having them leave us. Or if we have acute insecurities festering, we may fear that they will discover just how flawed and unlovable we really are.

If we aren't aware of this tendency, we may try to ward off this dreaded eventuality by trying to make ourselves appear flawless in the eyes of our beloved. We tell ourselves that if we look and act perfect, they won't have any reason to leave us. Although it may not feel that way, this is actually an attempt to control and manipulate the other person and limit their own power of choice. In other words, this is a behavior rooted in fear.

Just as often, the tide shifts the other way. As the heady chemicals of new love begin to wane, we may also find ourselves more and more preoccupied with fears about the person we're with: Is this person really who I think they are? Will this person really be everything I dreamed of? What if this person asks me for something I don't want to give? What if this person requires me to look at an aspect of myself that makes me uncomfortable, or nudges me to address an old wound I'd prefer to leave buried?

The same thing can happen with the love a parent feels for a child. When a baby is born, we feel carried along on a blissful tide of love for them. But as they grow up and begin to assert their own identity and make their own choices, that love can be complicated by fear. What if they behave in ways that are disrespectful? What if they get into trouble? What if we have differing views on how we each should live our lives?

When our love fails to magically dissolve these difficulties or make all our fears go away, we think there is something wrong with the relationship—but often we are the ones placing conditions on our love. Most of you probably have some idea of what I mean when I use the words *conditional* and *unconditional love*. But let's pause for just a moment and take a deeper dive into their significance.

When we practice unconditional love, we recognize that the nagual flows through all living beings and is present in all situations. Whether a person or situation is pleasant or unpleasant, easy or challenging, the nagual is still there, and through the eyes of unconditional love we are able to perceive it and honor it. In other words, whether your partner, child, neighbor, or even a stranger is acting in a way that you like or strongly dislike, the nagual is equally present, and the person is equally deserving of your love.

When you walk through a healthy forest, it's easy to see that all the various trees, grasses, bushes, and flowers are animated by the same life force. You can marvel at the beauty and diversity of the plant life around you, and can see how each part is integral to the whole. Being in the forest might fill you with a sense of beauty and harmony that hopefully stays with you long after you've returned to your typical surroundings. And learning to recognize the nagual in all beings and situations extends this beautiful feeling to all of life—this is the essence of unconditional love.

In contrast, conditional love is a state in which we struggle to perceive the nagual in certain people, qualities, or situations—or even insist that it can't possibly be there. You see the mess your cousin is making of her life and feel only judgment and blame; or you refuse to talk to your sister until she gives you a full apology for every last childhood incident about which you still feel bitter, and pays you back every last cent she owes you. Conditional love is often accompanied by strong feelings of righteousness and self-justification. The thought of extending kindness or forgiveness to that person feels outrageous and unfair, given the circumstances. We tell ourselves, *Of course I love her, but she needs to do this and this and this...*

Of course, the most common way we practice conditional love is with ourselves. We watch ourselves making social blunders, doing sloppy work, or failing to reach a goal, and think, *Pathetic! No wonder you haven't achieved this or accomplished that.* We see ourselves as projects to be completed or machines to be fixed, instead of living, breathing manifestations of the nagual.

My brother Jose went through a very difficult time in his youth, as he shares in his book *My Good Friend the Rattlesnake*, during which he struggled with drug addiction. This was a time of great fear for our entire family. We worried about him constantly, and often wished we could take away his power of choice because we were so afraid he was going to hurt himself or even die. Yet my father always insisted that we had to let Jose find his own way. We could offer our love, but we couldn't force him to live a life he didn't choose. My father saw the nagual in Jose even during his darkest moments. He modeled unconditional love through his commitment to acceptance instead of control.

Of course, this doesn't mean my father didn't draw boundaries on what was acceptable behavior, nor did it mean that he wasn't afraid of what might happen to Jose—but in both cases, he knew that putting his fear in charge wasn't going to help anyone. Quite the opposite: letting fear take the wheel would have made room for conditional love to sneak in—the kind of love that eventually says, *You are dear to me only if you do these things and stop doing those other things; if you fulfill my expectations and never hurt me.*

The opposite of fear isn't love in the way the word is commonly used; the opposite of fear is *unconditional* love. Acceptance. Empathy. In other words, the opposite of fear is a love that embraces discomfort, uncertainty, loss, and pain. Many of us believe we are practicing unconditional love, only to discover that we've been harboring conditions without even realizing it. When we feel the bliss of romance and falling in love, or when we hold our newborn child for the first time, we may imagine ourselves staying in this delightful state forever. When a difficulty arises, such as a betrayal, disappointment, or simple difference of opinion, we find that our blissful state of love has been invaded by anxiety, anger, and even resentment—all of which have their roots in fear.

Conditional love only sees what it wants to see, projecting an image onto life and the people we love of how we think they should be, and castigating them when they don't live up to our ideals. Unconditional love is the willingness to see the whole of life, including the people we love, as they actually are rather than how we might wish them to be.

Cultivating Unconditional Love

The ancient Greeks had a special word for unconditional love: *agape*. For them, this signified a type of love characterized by self-sacrifice and indifference to conditions—the type of love they imagined God having for human beings. Other traditions share similar ideas. The Bhagavad Gita describes unconditional love as devotion that doesn't waver in the face of distress or disappointment, and which is unattached to outcomes. The Buddhist word *metta* refers to a state of friendliness and goodwill toward all beings and all experiences, whether they are comfortable or uncomfortable, pleasant or unpleasant.

Unconditional love is a state that spiritual traditions have promoted and recognized as transformative for millennia. Yet these same traditions also acknowledge how difficult it can be to achieve such a state. We ascribe this type of love to gods, goddesses, and founders of spiritual and religious traditions, knowing how hard it can be to embody its ideals while inhabiting a human body and mind. We yearn to be capable of unconditional love, while wrestling with the very human experiences of jealousy, stress, and, yes, fear.

Knowing how difficult it can be to practice unconditional love, where do we begin? This is where our stalking-the-mind practice comes in again. Conditional love is often signaled by resistance on several levels. Maybe you feel a physical hardening of the heart when you're speaking with the person in question; maybe this physical hardening is accompanied by stories about how that person isn't trying hard enough, and by emotions of disappointment, frustration, and hurt. Zooming out, you can see that your whole being is steeling itself, perhaps out of fear of being hurt or taken advantage of.

The moment you realize that fear is driving your conditional love, everything changes. From the observer position, it's easy to see that hardening your heart or engaging in mental judgments isn't actually going to protect you, any more than clenching your hands on the steering wheel keeps you safe when you're driving a car. Conditional love may feel like self-protection or even inner strength, but when you look a little deeper, you discover it's all about fear. Ask yourself, *What am I protecting myself from? Which outcome do I think I can prevent by steeling myself in this way?*

Simply acknowledging that you feel scared and vulnerable can pave the way to feeling safe—and it's much easier to practice unconditional love when you feel safe than when you're feeling threatened. If you're driving a car on an icy road, it helps to be relaxed, focused, and present. The same is true of practicing unconditional love under challenging conditions that always arise in human relationships.

The Courage to Love

Unconditional love doesn't mean that you have no boundaries, and it doesn't mean that every action you take makes people happy. So often, we think that unconditional love means being a never-ending fountain of cheerfulness, approval, and affection for the people around us—presenting them with a perfect happy face that will in turn help them to be perfectly happy. But sometimes, unconditional love means taking an action that will upset the other person or even lead them to accuse you of harming them. (If you've ever tried to take a cookie away from a toddler with allergies, you know what I mean! In the case of a child with allergies, the correct action is clear and the resulting discomfort short-lived. But as we all know, this isn't always the case.)

I have a dear friend whose adult daughter was hooked on prescription drugs and marijuana. It was clear to everyone in the family that her substance use had become a problem, and after a couple years of putting up with erratic behavior and walking on eggshells around her, my friend approached his daughter and told her he believed she had developed an addiction. She vehemently disagreed.

My friend knew his daughter needed help, but he also knew that it was important not to make her feel judged or shamed, as she would only respond by pulling away. He decided to organize an intervention in which family members would join together to encourage her to go into rehab. However, he made sure everyone involved knew that the guiding principle for this intervention would be unconditional love.

On the day of the intervention, family members arrived at her apartment with letters they'd written, recounting the behavior and health changes they'd witnessed in her over the previous two years. In advance of the intervention, my friend had contacted a rehab center and arranged to take his daughter there if she agreed to go. After a tense meeting filled with tears from everyone present, his daughter agreed to go to rehab. My friend was overjoyed that the family had succeeded in convincing her while staying true to the principles of unconditional love.

Unfortunately, two days later his daughter withdrew herself from rehab, declaring that, unlike the "real" addicts at the rehab center, she did not have a problem. She resumed her drug use, and my friend was left to puzzle over what unconditional love would have him do next. As of this writing, she is still active in her addiction. Like my father was with Jose, my friend is still committed to interacting with his daughter from a place of unconditional love. For him, this means setting clear boundaries on when and how he sees her, including not doing so when she is obviously under the influence or acting erratically. He is careful not to shame her when he does see her and also attends support groups for family members of those with addictions. He stays open with his own feelings of sadness and loss and shares them with others when they arise but also reminds himself that his daughter is on her own path, that the universal nagual and the nagual inside her are watching over her, and that whatever happens will ultimately be for the good of all involved.

Like my friend, there will be times when you're dealing with an intense situation, emotions are running high, and the best course of action isn't always clear. In situations like these, you can always pause and ask yourself, is what I am about to do or say coming from a place of unconditional love or a place of fear? If the answer is fear, do your best to refrain, even if it means doing nothing. Give your nervous system time to settle down, do what you can to establish a sense of safety inside yourself, and try not to speak or act until you can do so from a place of unconditional love.

As any parent knows, and as my friend's experience demonstrates, unconditional love sometimes conflicts with being liked. In some cases, unconditional love requires you to stand firm when you believe you are doing what's right, and not give in to what others say they want. When you create and enforce boundaries with loved ones, you may have to accept some discomfort or even pain. Even harder, you may have to accept the fact that you can't force another person to understand or see things your way, and you can't change the story they tell about you inside their own head.

In moments like these, it's important to remember the ways that trust is core to unconditional love. I sometimes say that the opposite of fear isn't love, it's trust—something we will discuss in detail in the next chapter. Even if it doesn't seem like things will work out from where you're standing right now, trust can help you stay the course, knowing that the nagual will find a way.

While things may not seem harmonious or fair right away, in the unfolding of time, we can trust that the seeds of unconditional love will come to fruition. Our job is to plant them. Trusting life gives us the freedom to love unconditionally, and the patience to let the results of our actions unfold. And while you may feel a temporary twinge of fear when you take benevolent action that upsets another person, you can trust that your efforts will someday sprout in a way you least expect.

Exercise: Falling in Love with Life

It's easy to fall in love with the pleasant aspects of life—such as meeting a wonderful new person, enjoying delicious food, or moving into a nice home. But few of us realize that we can also fall in love with the uncomfortable aspects of our experience, knowing that they often contain hidden blessings we do not yet understand.

Think of an experience you associate with fear—for example, having dental work done, getting stuck in traffic, struggling with insomnia, or confronting a family member about a sensitive topic. Now bathe this experience in love. In your thoughts, words, and actions, treat it as if it's an opportunity instead of a scourge you'd just as soon do away with. Allow yourself to consider the most wonderful possible outcome of undergoing this experience. Allow yourself to feel gratitude for the benefits this experience could potentially bring into your life. What changes in your body and mind when you dissolve your resistance to the uncomfortable aspects of life, and love them unconditionally?

Exercise: Loving Without Fear

Think of a person you are very afraid of losing—for example, your partner, your child, or your best friend.

Now, imagine that this person is living a completely different life that doesn't include you. For example, you might imagine that your partner is married to someone else, living in a different city, with a different job. Imagine this person being blissfully happy in this alternate life. Go way overboard, giving this person a life in which their every wish is fulfilled. Notice that your ability to imagine the perfect life for this person springs from your love for them. Notice if any anxiety you feel about losing them is overcome by happiness for them, as you imagine them experiencing this perfect life.

Just as you can imagine a happy life for your partner or friend that does not involve you, know that you, too, can experience happiness and love in an infinite variety of possible futures, whether or not that person is around forever, and whether or not your life takes the shape you hoped.

Exercise: Holding on to Love

Make a list of all the people in your life who have shown you love. Include people with whom you have long-standing relationships, such as your parents or spouse, but also old friends and acquaintances with whom you have lost touch, and strangers with whom you crossed paths for only a moment, but who brightened your day in some memorable way.

Chances are you've already had the experience of losing someone's love, if only because you knew the person in question for a short time, or barely knew them at all. Whether you consciously realized it or not, you moved on from that loss and found love again and again. And of course, it's also true that the love you received from them, either for a day or a lifetime, was never lost. It still lives in your heart when you remember it or call it to mind.

How does it feel to recognize the fact that a relationship can change or end and yet you can still feel the love? Can you tune in to the unconditional love that exists in this moment, rather than seeing love as a possession or past experience to which you must cling? This is the love coming from inside of you. Just like your mind and body only exist because you are here to give them life, your love exists because you do. Without you, none of it exists. You are the source of love in your life.

Chapter Six

Trust and Temachia

If you've ever tried to quit a habit like biting your nails or scrolling on your phone, it probably wasn't long before you realized that you had to give yourself something else to do with your hands, whether that was solving crossword puzzles, knitting, or weeding the yard. The same is true of fear. As we become aware of our psychological fears and ultimately release them, it's important to replace those fears with something else—otherwise, we risk leaving a void where fear can easily sneak back in. Therefore, as we work to dismantle unnecessary psychological fear, we must also establish a powerful presence in its place: unshakeable faith in ourselves and in life.

For some of us, the word *faith* is burdened with religious connotations, or associated with wishful thinking and a denial of science. I've also had apprentices over the years bristle at any mention of the word because they grew up in a home that used faith as a primary tool for domestication, replete with fear, guilt, and punishment for anyone who dared to question it.

For this reason, I want to be clear that in the Toltec tradition, faith refers to complete and unconditional trust in life and trust in yourself rather than blind adherence to any particular religion or creed. The question then becomes, what do I mean by trusting in life and yourself?

In explaining the role of trust, I can think of no better example than my grandmother, Madre Sarita, a well-known curandera, or faith healer, who founded and ran a widely respected healing center in San Diego for many years. She was so well-regarded for her ability to help heal people that she was written about in newspapers, interviewed by the local NBC affiliate, and was eventually inducted into the San Diego Women's Hall of Fame, one year before her death in 2008 at the age of ninety-eight.

But that is only half of her story.

Sarita was born in 1910 in the village of Juanacatlán, Jalisco, in south-central Mexico. At the age of fourteen, she was married and went to work in a textile factory; by fifteen, she had given birth to the first of thirteen children, whom she raised while continuing to work in a succession of low-paying factory jobs. Sarita's grandfather, don Exiquio, was a nagual in the Toltec tradition. Although he had given her training in our family's lineage when she was a child, by the time she was married and working she had little time or interest in the practices of our ancestors. She and her husband moved to the city, and her children pursued educations and careers in science and medicine—a far cry from the Toltec tradition Sarita had grown up with.

In her fifties, however, Sarita had a health crisis that initiated a whole new chapter in her life. She had developed chest pains and a heart murmur, the cause of which proved to be gallstones. The surgery proposed by doctors at that time was very risky, and as an alternative, Sarita's mother urged her to visit a temple of spiritual healing. Sarita was skeptical. By then, she'd been thoroughly entrenched in a Western, materialist worldview for several decades. She asked herself, *If the doctors can't help me, what can these ignorant people do?* Still, she decided to visit the temple.

There, she met a healer named Petra Castro, who suggested that Sarita undergo what he called "psychic surgery," a form of energy healing in which no actual cutting of the body is done. Again, Sarita was skeptical: How could Petra do anything about her gallstones without literally removing them? This wasn't real medicine, just smoke and mirrors. Still, her condition was getting worse, and at the insistence of her mother and with few downsides to attempting it, she agreed to the procedure.

During the psychic surgery, Sarita fell into a kind of trance in which she saw a doctor and nurse operating on her body and removing the gallstones. She could even hear each individual gallstone make a pinging sound as the doctor dropped it onto a plate. The visions were so convincing that when the surgery was over, she couldn't believe that her gallstones hadn't literally been removed. She went on to make a full recovery, and the experience changed her. She decided to become Petra's apprentice, and she also returned to study our Toltec tradition with her father, don Leonardo, also a nagual in the Toltec tradition. When her apprenticeship was complete, she dedicated the rest of her life to healing others using similar techniques, eventually establishing the healing center in San Diego, where she treated hundreds of people every year.

As a teenager, I often acted as my grandmother's translator when she taught classes, gave sermons, or performed faith healings. I was always struck by the absolute confidence with which Madre Sarita performed her work. It was clear to me that she fully expected her healings to have their intended result. Not only that, but she trusted that her intent mattered; indeed, that it could affect the very course of reality. At the end of every healing session, she would close her prayers by saying, "*Así sea, así se haga, y así será*," which translates to "May it be so, so it will be made, so it shall be."

Even at a young age, I could see the calming impact she had on her patients—their bodies visibly relaxing at the suggestion that the healing they longed for would soon come to pass. Although some of the people who showed up at her clinic were initially skeptical, saying things like "I don't really believe in this" and "I'm only here because my spouse insisted," things changed when Sarita began to do her work. Their fear and resistance seemed to melt in the presence of her quiet and skillful manner.

One time, early in my training, I asked her a question. "How come some people still get better even if they don't have faith or belief that what you're doing will help?" Her answer surprised me. She said that at some level they were open to being healed, even if they claimed not to be—otherwise they wouldn't have come at all. She explained that even if their conscious mind doubted it, the fact that they showed up demonstrated that some part of them did believe it was possible. "It is our actions that matter, not what we say," she told me—a truth I have realized over and over in my own life.

The Placebo Effect

Most of you are probably familiar with the placebo effect—the phenomenon by which a percentage of patients in a clinical trial improve even if they unknowingly received a sugar pill instead of the "real" medicine. In fact, the placebo effect is so well documented that the vast majority of new drugs are required to include a placebo control in their studies when seeking FDA approval. While pharmaceutical companies have been bringing new drugs to market using placebo testing for the past hundred years, they've also inadvertently proven the power of the human mind to heal.

The placebo effect demonstrates that simply believing that we are taking a medicine or receiving a treatment can make us feel better. In some cases, this belief can even cure us. In the case of Madre Sarita's healing work, she frequently prescribed some combination of herbal medicine or physical therapy along with the purely spiritual elements of her work—but it was the patient's own trust in the healing process that played the biggest role in their recovery. She often told me that it was not *her* healing the patients, but their own faith through the action of giving themselves permission to heal. "I am just a channel."

In medical trials, some patients given a placebo will improve even when they claim not to believe that they are going to get better. Like the skeptics in Madre Sarita's office, we can say one thing while experiencing something completely different on the level of the unconscious. No matter how skeptical you claim to be, the fact is that you showed up and received the treatment. This hints at the fact that some part of you believes it will work, even if you don't have conscious access to that part. At the end of the day, it's our actions that matter, not what we say or even think.

The same is true in all areas of life—take this book, for example. Right now, you may not believe that it is possible to overcome your psychological fears, or find your own personal freedom, or make some other needed change in your life. You may even be expressing strong doubts to your friends, therapist, or anyone who will listen. But the fact remains that despite these surface-level objections, something in you still led you to pick up this book and read it. Some part of you is taking action, even if your thoughts and words are expressing resistance. Some part of you trusts that the exercises and practices in this book will help you—otherwise you wouldn't be here—and that trust is what I want to talk about next.

Universal Trust

In the English language, the word *trust* usually refers to a belief in the truth or reliability of a fact, statement, person, or idea: "I *trust* my brother's judgment" or "I *trust* the results of that study." In Nahuatl, the word for trust is *temachia*, and I think of it as a universal trust in life. It refers to the conviction I have that if we have the right intention in our heart, even in the midst of great difficulty, things will work out for the ultimate good of all involved.

Chances are you've already encountered the concept of temachia by another name. Some people call it "trusting in God," "trusting the universe," or "trusting the dharma or the way things are." I would propose that every time you think of the word *temachia*, let it remind you to place absolute trust in the nagual: the life force that animates all beings, and which is with us at every moment of our lives, both during the peak experiences and the moments of sorrow and despair.

Have you ever gone outside on a starry night and marveled at the perfection of the cosmos, or watched a documentary about space and been amazed by beautiful images of our galaxy? Isn't it incredible that the *very same force* that produced a spiral nebula is also present and at work in your very own life? In moments like these, we can easily be flooded with a sense of temachia, in which our ordinary fears and worries drop away, and we recognize the utter perfection of the nagual.

In this way, temachia isn't just an intellectual idea, but a cosmic principle—almost like a law of physics. It's the unwavering knowledge that we are held in a web of relationships as vast as the universe itself. Even though the meaning of individual events isn't always readily apparent to us, we nevertheless trust that we are being led in a positive direction, and that our lives are being shaped by the nagual for a higher purpose. Chances are you've had some experience in your life that at the time felt like a setback, but which later proved to be a tremendous gift. That is the proof of temachia.

Cultivating temachia doesn't mean that you blithely sail through life, impervious to any sorrow, hardship, or disappointment. It means that you can see those temporary difficulties from a higher perspective: as opportunities to grow in love and wisdom, while remaining firmly anchored to your highest values and intent. It also makes you more loving and accepting of other people, whether or not you agree with their opinions or their behavior; after all, the nagual is unfolding in them just as perfectly as it is unfolding in you. In the words of the astronomer Carl Sagan, "Every one of us is, in the cosmic perspective, precious. If a human disagrees with you, let him live. In a hundred billion galaxies, you will not find another."

Living from a state of temachia can radically change what you expect from life, and therefore what you experience. When your mind is dominated by fear and distrust, you may unconsciously be steeling yourself for experiences of abandonment, humiliation, scarcity, and loss. This state of negative expectation can affect you on all levels, from tensed muscles in your body to guarded interactions with other people. We all know someone who is always waiting for the other shoe to drop or the axe to fall—the friend who expects his girlfriend to break up with him and so refrains from investing too much in the relationship, or the wealthy relative who saves every penny just in case her fortunes change. Sometimes these fears and the behaviors they produce create a self-fulfilling prophecy—and even when they don't, just think of all the unhappiness that occurs from living this way.

When you shift from fear to *universal trust*, the opposite is true. You can relax—physically, mentally, and emotionally—knowing that everything is going to work out for the best, even if you're not sure how that will look, and even when it's not how you had hoped. You can truly appreciate people for who they are, instead of worrying about all the ways they may someday hurt you. You can do acts of service for others and for the world, trusting that your own needs will also be met. You can live your life with the expectation that abundance, love, and connection will find you wherever you are.

Although my grandmother grew up poor with little formal education, she was rich in temachia. She trusted that her own children would receive an education and even pursue advanced degrees, and sure enough, they did. Although she arrived in the United States as an undocumented immigrant, she expected to receive the assistance she needed to become a citizen, and indeed she did. Although many of the patients who flowed through her healing center had seemingly intractable problems, she expected them to get better, and many times they did. When I asked her how she had achieved such incredible things after such humble beginnings, she answered, "I have 100 percent faith in the power of life." To this day, Madre Sarita's answer is the best definition of temachia I have ever heard.

One Hundred Percent Faith in Life

Think back on the toughest challenges you've faced—illnesses, injuries, family dramas, relationship struggles, moments when you thought your life was over. If you are reading this book, it means you're alive—and if you're alive, it means that you've survived 100 percent of everything that has ever happened to you, no matter how difficult or frightening it might have been. Maybe you survived thanks to your intelligence and resourcefulness; maybe you survived thanks to the kindness and protection of people around you; or maybe you survived out of apparent luck, or by some combination of all of those factors. The point is, the nagual found a way to flow through you in such a way that you survived.

Although we all have our plans and to-do lists, the fact is that much of life takes place outside of our control. Just think of the last time you tripped or fell. I'm going to guess that your arms instinctively shot out to catch yourself before you were even conscious of it. The fact that we will instinctively grab a tree root to keep ourselves from falling off a cliff is proof that at the most primitive of levels, we can trust ourselves. And if we can trust ourselves to break a physical fall, maybe we can trust ourselves at higher levels — maybe we can even trust ourselves absolutely.

If you reviewed the story of your life, you could probably find hundreds of examples of times when you took an action that was positive and protective, whether you consciously intended to or not: times when you sought food or shelter, when you found friends and mentors, when you instinctively avoided dangerous situations, or when you reached for an opportunity that catapulted you into a better mode of existence. Those are all examples of ways the nagual was working through you. Indeed, when patients showed up at Madre Sarita's temple claiming they "didn't really believe" in her treatments but were going to try them anyway, that was the nagual working through them!

Life wants to persist through us; life wants us to thrive in all kinds of ways. Otherwise, life wouldn't have bothered to give us a survival instinct at all, let alone qualities like intelligence, kindness, and compassion. Once you realize that life itself is on your side, everything changes. The question shifts from "How do I survive?" to "What can I give?" When you have 100 percent faith in life, you can stop putting your energy into fear-based strategies for shoring up your defenses and invest that energy into crafting the life you want to live—and making the world a better place for you and others to live in.

My grandmother didn't discover her life's work until she was in her fifties, but once she opened her temple, Madre Sarita carried on her healing mission until her death at the age of ninety-eight. By that point, she had no need for money as her family was able to take care of themselves; indeed, she often treated patients who had no ability to pay. Her complete trust in life had brought her to a point where she could devote herself to service, leaving the basic survival needs of her youth far behind.

Madre Sarita is far from the only example of a person who was able to do incredible things thanks to their faith in life. At the age of twenty-six, Chuck Collins, the heir to the Oscar Mayer wiener fortune, donated his inheritance to a handful of funds for social change. Unlike many people in his position, he trusted that his life had a higher purpose than simply maximizing his personal wealth. He went on to publish several books about wealth inequality, and encouraged other people born into extreme wealth to ally themselves with common people and consider the needs of the poor.

The actor Jim Carrey was born into a working-class family for whom financial precarity was constant, and in high school he was forced to work overnight shifts as a janitor in exchange for his family's housing. However, he knew that he was extraordinarily talented at doing impressions and making people laugh. He found ways to cultivate this talent, performing in small venues whenever he got the chance. In a move that would become the stuff of legend, he wrote himself a check for ten million dollars for "acting services rendered" and carried it around in his wallet—an expression of his faith that life would find a way for him to share his gift with the world. Sure enough, his temachia led him to become the famous actor we know today.

Of course, most people who have an abundance of temachia aren't rich or famous, nor do they care to be. In fact, I'm sure you know people in your life right now who live with temachia as a guiding principle in their lives, but you may or may not have noticed. They may call it by another name, simply trusting the universe, faith, or something else. They are not hard to find once you open your eyes and look. These trusting souls are helpful to others, they lean into the positive in any situation, and while they may still feel psychological fear from time to time, they don't let that fear control their lives.

When we have 100 percent faith in life, we are free to focus on our highest values instead of fretting over minor fluctuations in our personal comfort and status. Fear is always telling us to settle for less, but trust allows us to pursue the aspirations and take the actions that lead to a truly meaningful life. Whether you call it trust, faith, or temachia, this quality of conviction is essential for banishing psychological fear from your mind. In the exercises that follow, you will learn some powerful tools to help you establish this sense of conviction in your own life.

Exercise: Being Your Own Faith Healer

Although you may never meet a faith healer in real life, you can practice being your own faith healer by intentionally cultivating positive qualities in your mind.

The next time you get sick, spend a few minutes imagining yourself in perfect health. You might visualize yourself going for a run, playing with your kids, or tinkering on a project. Call to mind the sensations of vigor and vitality.

The next time you feel worried about a tricky problem at work, spend a few minutes imagining yourself tackling this problem with ease and coming up with a wonderful solution. Call the energy of inspiration and creativity into your mind and body and visualize your success in detail.

Anytime you feel fear or anxiety, visualize the best possible outcome to the fearful situation, and consciously invoke whichever emotions or qualities you would most like to feel.

By practicing in this way, you are training your mind and body to expect a positive outcome, the same way faith healers like Madre Sarita plant positive expectations in their patients' minds as a way of helping them heal. Over time, your mind and body will learn to expect only good things from life, and fewer mental and physical resources will go toward resistance and fear.

Exercise: Expanding the Circle of Trust

No matter how much fear or anxiety you may feel, chances are there at least a few ways in which you already do trust in life. For example, maybe you've always believed in the kindness of strangers, or you've figured out that you can always find a way to support yourself, thanks to your education and skills. Even though you may have no way of proving that a kindly stranger will always show up to help you out of a jam, or that you'll always be able to make a living in any economy, your trust in these aspects of life has an enormous influence on your confidence in life, as well as the risks you allow yourself to take.

In this exercise, I invite you to expand this circle of trust to encompass the aspects of your life that are currently dominated by fear.

First, take out a piece of paper and a pen. Next, draw two large, nonintersecting circles. Label one circle "trust" and the other "fear."

In the "trust" circle, write down the areas of your life in which you already feel a great deal of trust: for example, your friendships, your work, or even big concepts like "goodness" or "the divine." Simply paying attention to the ways in which you already practice trust can make it easier for you to trust even more.

In the "fear" circle, write down areas of your life that are currently ruled by fear: perhaps your finances, your relationship with your siblings, or your personal appearance.

Now, take out a second piece of paper. This time, draw only a single large circle, and label it "trust." Look at the words you originally assigned to your "fear" circle, and if you choose to do so, copy them down into this circle instead. Remember, you always have the power of your yes and your no.

If you choose yes, imagine what it would be like to have absolute faith that these aspects of your life are going to work out in wonderful ways. What would it be like if you trusted absolutely that you would always have enough, that you would always be enough, and that the universe was ultimately benevolent? Would such a perspective allow you to do more good with your life and devote yourself to a higher purpose? How much impact could you make on the world if you truly had faith that you would always be okay?

Keep your new "trust" circle in a place you can see it. Anytime you experience fear or anxiety about a specific aspect of life, make a point of adding it to your circle of trust.

Chapter Seven

Embracing Uncertainty

A friend of mine was on his way to an important business meeting when his connecting flight was grounded in a storm. As he wandered through the airport, powerless to change his situation, his mind prickled with anxiety. What would happen if he couldn't close this deal? Who would he be if he didn't succeed at this? A lot had led up to this, as it had taken him years to get to the point where he could meet with this high-powered client; what if this type of opportunity never came up again?

He had recently gotten divorced, and focusing on work had helped him get through the loss. He poured his time and energy into developing himself as a professional and hitting the career milestones that had come more slowly before. Now, his mind provided him with stories of going back home with his tail between his legs, having missed his "one chance" at success, and of the lonely and unfulfilling future he now had to face.

But shortly after he returned to the seating area, coffee in hand, a beautiful woman sat down across from him and struck up a conversation. It turned out they came from the same hometown and even had old friends in common. They were even reading the same book! Although he didn't yet realize it, he had just met his future wife.

Many of us have an unconscious belief that if we could only control life we wouldn't be afraid anymore. Instead of feeling open, curious, or even excited when life doesn't go according to our plans, many of us have a mental habit of feeling affronted and dismayed. Deep down, most of us believe that *we* are the most qualified human being on earth to determine what should be happening—even though for most of us, some of what we call the "best" things that ever happened to us came in a way we never could have predicted, much less controlled.

When his plane was grounded, my friend's mind insisted that this was a terrible thing that would have a negative impact on his life. Yet it proved to be a wonderful thing in ways he never could have predicted. Although he missed his business meeting, he found his life partner and the mother of his children. Far from losing out, he gained the life of his dreams. His story is a wonderful example of the importance of temachia.

My friend's experience confirms that the unknown contains great gifts for us, ones that we would miss if we were in charge of everything. Although human beings are blessed with wonderful imaginations, we often limit our imaginations to a relatively small sphere. We think about events that happened recently, or scenarios that are easy for our minds to conjure, instead of considering the entire scope of possibility. Psychologists refer to this as the "availability heuristic"—the tendency to reach for what's convenient, making snap judgments based on our limited experience while ignoring the rich, sparkling, and infinitely creative manifestations of the nagual.

The truth is that uncertainty contains the potential for wonderful things to happen, not just bad things. Yet when faced with uncertainty, the mind's typical default state is fear. No matter how many times our fearful predictions are proven wrong, we nevertheless relinquish a great deal of energy to elaborating on these predictions and even mentally rehearsing them, until it feels like we've lived through stressful events that were entirely imaginary. As Mark Twain wrote, "I've lived through some terrible things in my life, some of which have actually happened." And as a friend of mine likes to say, "Ninety-nine percent of my worst days never happened, except in my own mind."

Recently, I went through an experience that illustrated this phenomenon to a tee. My doctor ordered some routine blood tests, which came back showing elevated markers that might indicate leukemia, a form of cancer. Over the next few minutes, my mind immediately went to my wife and children. I would have to prepare them for my death; I would have to talk to my lawyer, review my will, and make sure all my affairs were in order. I would need to figure out a long-term plan for my son, to ensure he would receive the best possible care. Not only that, but I would have to break the news to my friends and extended family, and support them through the anguish they would feel over my impending death.

Even though the blood test was far from conclusive, my mind nevertheless reached for the worst outcome that was available: *Test equals cancer. Cancer equals death. Death equals bad.* As my training kicked in and I began to stalk my mind, it occurred to me that following this train of thought made me feel like I was in control, even though it meant collapsing my worldview to include only the most extreme possibility. In other words, it felt *safer* to believe that I was about to die because there was certainty attached to that thought. The fact was that my likelihood of having leukemia was low—I have no family history, and the test result could easily be explained by an infection—yet like many humans, my sense of reason and logic isn't always a match for the power of fear-based thoughts and the emotions they produce.

After getting further tests, it turned out that I didn't have cancer after all, but a condition called monoclonal B-cell lymphocytosis. Although I was grateful for the opportunity to reflect on my own mortality, the truth was that I had lived through a harrowing battle with cancer in my mind—one that never actually happened. Instead, the vast uncertainty of life had provided something entirely different: an opportunity to watch my own mind going through a cycle of fear and coming out on the other side.

You may have come across the statistic that most people are more afraid of public speaking than they are of death. Uncertainty can feel so frightening that we may be willing to do almost anything to end it, even if that means leaping to a conclusion that isn't in our best interest. We would rather "know" something terrible than remain in a space of unknowing, and that can lead us to bring all kinds of drama into our lives.

Learning to Trust

As you learn the practice of temachia, you will likely find that there are domains in life in which you are more comfortable with uncertainty than in others. For example, you may be confident in your ability to navigate unexpected challenges at work, but feel that you need total control and predictability when it comes to your relationships with others. You may have no fear at all about losing your job, but an intense fear of your partner leaving you. These are important things to notice, because we try the hardest to control the things we fear most.

A friend of mine used to experience intense social anxiety. In the rare event she would invite friends over to her home for a visit, she always felt like she needed a plan to entertain them. She would pore over events listings in the newspaper and even buy board games and puzzles to make sure that nobody was ever bored or at loose ends. When it came to spending time with people, she wasn't sure how to handle unstructured time, and so she planned everything out in advance to make sure this anxiety-provoking situation would never arise.

Then one day, some friends called to say they were coming to town that very evening and asked if they could stay at her place for the weekend. Although she said yes, my friend quietly panicked. She hadn't had time to plan! Not only that, but she was in the middle of a big art project and her place was a mess. As she waited for her friends to arrive, she frantically looked for concerts, events, and exhibits she could take them to see. But after an hour of doing so, her stalking practice kicked in, and she made a decision to trust that everything would work out, even if she couldn't see how.

As it turns out, when her friends showed up, there was yet another surprise: they were both recovering from the flu, and while they were no longer contagious, they had almost no energy to do the activities she had hastily planned. Instead, she made a big pot of ginger tea, and they alternated between slow, meandering conversations and watching nature documentaries. In the evening, she cooked a big pot of soup and tucked her friends in with blankets on the couch. Although she could never have predicted it, taking care of them in this way was much more meaningful than any of the activities she would have planned had she been in control.

This experience completely changed my friend's relationship with socializing. She realized she could trust that positive experiences would emerge naturally from her interactions with others. She no longer had the same fear when faced with an unstructured, unplanned visit. In fact, she began to look forward to unplanned visits because she enjoyed being surprised and inspired rather than knowing exactly what was going to happen.

Attempting to control outcomes in life is ultimately an illusion, albeit a persistent one. The truth is that there are always thousands or even millions of factors at play, ranging from the weather to traffic to random chance to historical and political conditions that are far too complex to list. But sometimes our attempts at control appear to work, just often enough that we pat ourselves on the back for "successfully" causing them. We take credit when our attempts at control go well—and when they don't go well, we often blame it on outside factors, failing to realize that control itself is the problem.

In the Toltec tradition, we say that attempts at control are always rooted in fear. The mind pushes us into staying within our self-imposed limits instead of trusting that things will work out in the end. To address this fear, we practice awareness, notice when we are trying to control something, and recommit to trusting the power of the universe. When you become a master at this, you notice that many things turn out better when you resist the urge to control everything—sometimes even much, much better than they would have if you had been in control of the outcome. It is often in the unknown where true transformation occurs.

When my brother Jose and I take our apprentices on power journeys to the pyramids in Teotihuacan, we don't provide them with a schedule. Instead, we explain that we teach and lead from the heart, and prefer to leave space for transformative experiences to unfold instead of rushing off to the next activity or destination on the list. Some of the apprentices have a very hard time with this! They feel very anxious not knowing exactly what's going to happen or when; in the mornings, they want to ask a hundred questions about the events of the day, and they get even more worried when Jose and I tell them we don't know.

In some cases, these apprentices add to their suffering by piling on self-judgment and self-recrimination for their struggle with uncertainty. They say things like, "I'm such a stick-in-the-mud, I can never just go with the flow," or "I wish I could be spontaneous like everyone else, but I guess I'm just too high-strung." They apologize for their fearful behavior and feel shame at the ways that the need for control has colonized their lives—never mind the fact that they were probably domesticated to be this way. It's nothing personal. If you look around, it's easy to see that there is little our culture currently wants more than control. It feels powerful, it's elusive, and not everyone can have it at once.

When this happens, Jose and I always try to guide them back to a place of unconditional self-love. After all, the need for control springs from a desire to protect yourself—and if you want to protect yourself, it means you must love yourself, even if you don't realize it. In that sense, getting in touch with your fear can be a bridge to the love that is already within you. When viewed through this lens, our fear of uncertainty is simply love that has yet to reach its highest expression—a beautiful potential, and nothing to be ashamed of at all.

It can take a few days for the anxiety to wear off, but when it does, something miraculous happens. The very same apprentices who showed up every morning looking anxious and asking "What are we doing today?" become relaxed and radiant. They stop looking at their watches. And at the end of the journey, they often say their favorite activities were the spontaneous rituals and ceremonies that *none* of us could have planned. Watching these apprentices let go of their desire for control and embrace the unknown always warms my heart and reminds me why I love teaching.

Exercise: Predicting the Good

Think of a subject that causes you anxiety: for example, family relationships, finances, climate change, or politics. Now make a list of ten unexpectedly good things that might happen that are completely outside your control. For example, new technologies might emerge, new people might come onto the scene, and new opportunities might arise that could completely change the situation. Allow your imagination to run wild. Consciously push back against the availability heuristic by reaching for ideas that don't fall within the usual repertoire of your imagination.

As you build your list, notice any changes in your mind, body, and mood. Do you start to feel energized as you contemplate new possibilities? Do you feel excited, rather than daunted, when you consider the unknown? How might you apply this practice to other areas of your life throughout your day, until it becomes a habit to consider challenges as opportunities for change rather than the end of the world?

Exercise: Exploring Uncertainty

Think of an area of your life in which you are very uncomfortable with uncertainty—for example, social interactions, your finances, or travel. Next, take out a pen and paper, and write down the specific fears you have about this topic. For example, if you've chosen travel, you might note that you're afraid of getting lost, having to sleep somewhere uncomfortable, or missing out on sights and experiences that you could have otherwise enjoyed if you had carefully planned.

Now, choose a context in which you will face this fear. For example, decide that you will leave one day of your vacation completely unplanned, that you will sketch out a budget for the next few weeks but leave some room for spontaneous fun, or that you will invite friends over with no plan for how to entertain them.

When the day comes, remind yourself that *some* aspects of your experience are going to be uncomfortable. There may be moments of awkwardness, frustration, or anxiety. Do your best to accept this discomfort as the "price of admission" for making friends with uncertainty.

At the end of the day, review what happened with an eye for the positive. What did you do or experience that would not have been possible had you stuck to a script? What were the very best moments of the day? Did you feel proud, surprised, moved, or even thrilled?

Recall these positive emotions the next time you find yourself in a habitual pattern of trying to eliminate uncertainty.

Exercise: Saying Thank You to Fear

Sometimes, the very best way to release our fearful tendencies is to express our appreciation for the ways this fear has protected us. Instead of getting angry or frustrated at our fear, we can acknowledge the fact that this fear has a positive reason for existing.

First, think of an area in your life in which you feel the greatest need for control and predictability—for example, your social interactions. Now, imagine your fear is a dear friend who is doing everything in their power to help you and protect you. Make a list of all the well-meaning actions this friend is doing on your behalf. For example, "Making sure my friends and family have a good time, so they'll want to spend more time with me," or "Making sure social interactions don't get too chaotic in order to protect me from burnout." Instead of beating yourself up for your fearful tendencies, honor the very real and significant ways these fears have protected you from harm. This will make it much easier to gently shift from resisting uncertainty to embracing it.

Chapter Eight

The Divided Mind

One day, a friend of mine was hiking with his mother in Sedona, Arizona, when his mother lost her footing, tumbled down the path, and landed on a sharp rock. She was in severe pain from the fall and was having trouble breathing. Fortunately, my friend had cell service and dialed 911. They dispatched a helicopter, and when it arrived the medics who examined her were concerned about possible damage to her internal organs. They placed his mom on a stretcher and prepared to transport her to the hospital.

When my friend approached the helicopter, expecting to fly to the hospital with her, the pilot stopped him. "There's only room for your mother," he said. "Not you."

My friend's mind reeled as he realized that he would have to make the long hike back to his car and then drive two hours to the hospital in Flagstaff with no way of knowing how his mother was doing. After the helicopter took off, he began to hike quickly, practically jogging down the trail and nearly stumbling on a rock himself. His mind raced with countless stories about how his mother might be critically injured or even dead by the time he reached her.

Luckily, my friend was an experienced meditator. He soon recognized that his mind was getting away from him, and he made a strong internal decision to focus on the present moment. He began by slowing down his pace, noticing the landscape around him, and focusing on each breath. When he got to his car, he paid attention to the feeling of the steering wheel under his hands and the mile markers posted along the side of the highway. By consciously placing his attention on his sensory experience and his immediate environment, he quieted down his mitote, reconnected to his sense of temachia, and took back his power. When he finally got to the hospital, he found that while his mother had broken some ribs, her injuries were not life-threatening, and she soon made a full recovery.

In the modern world, it is considered admirable and indeed necessary to multitask. We take phone calls while doing the dishes, or power through our backlog of emails while watching the news. Although this multitasking may save us time in some cases, it also leads to a mind that is divided and has trouble focusing on just one thing at a time. Just as a muscle will atrophy when it's not used, the same thing happens to the mind when we don't exercise it effectively. Before long, we may even believe that we don't have the ability to focus our minds—that they just go where they want, and nothing we do can change that.

When the mind loses its ability to focus, it leaves us more vulnerable to fear, as we have no idea how to rein in our minds when they begin to wander off into nightmarish story-making tendencies. The modern world can lead us to believe that more is better—more stuff, more thinking, more feverish information-seeking—when in fact we already have much more than we can possibly use. The practice of focusing the mind on one thing at a time doesn't get much mention in the modern world, but it's an important factor in combatting persistent fear.

In my family's Toltec tradition, the art of focused attention has long been a tool for mind training. As part of our training, my father and grandmother would ask my brother and me to choose a song to listen to on the stereo, and then focus on only one instrument for the entire track. We weren't allowed to choose the singer's voice, because that was too easy—instead, we had to choose the bass, the drums, or the guitar and keep our focus exclusively on that instrument for the entire song. If our attention wandered to the lyrics or got hooked by any other instrument, we had to restart the song and try again until we could listen to the whole track without losing our focus on the one instrument.

Later, I discovered the power of meditation and stalking the mind for building my awareness and developing my ability to focus. Whether it's sitting cross-legged and watching my breath or going for a long run outdoors and focusing on the rhythm of my footfalls, meditation helps create a space between the voices in my mitote and the nagual that is always observing them.

When something unexpected happens that produces fear in us, if we aren't able to focus the mind we are far more likely to react to the event rather than respond to it, propelled by whatever thought or emotion happens to be at the forefront of our mind at that moment. The bigger the fear, the bigger the reaction. However, if we are practiced at stalking the mind, we are much more likely to respond rather than react to the things that trigger us.

Fear-based reactions almost always cause us to say or do things we later regret.

Although we may tell ourselves that our reactions were deliberate and calculated—indeed, that we could not have responded any other way—in truth this is rarely the case. With the help of focus, we gain access to a wider range of potential responses, instead of letting the biggest and loudest voice in the mitote determine our actions every time.

When a fearful thought occurs and our mind isn't practiced at staying focused, it is more likely to be overrun with dire potential outcomes. This can happen in our Personal Dream, as when my friend began to imagine that his mother was critically injured. If we aren't careful, this tendency will not only cause fear to proliferate inside us, but it can also sow seeds of fear in the people around us. When we speak with care and accuracy, sticking to the facts, we are less likely to sow unnecessary fear in others or nurture fear in ourselves.

Fear and Gossip

It's clear that in the current Dream of the Planet, many humans *like* to be scared, in one way or another. While there is nothing inherently wrong with going to a horror movie or tuning in to the latest TV drama, other activities we engage in can be far less benign. For example, we live in a culture in which almost every news headline is designed to garner as much attention and anxiety as possible. For many, fear-provoking gossip isn't even considered a bad habit, but simply normal, everyday conversation.

If we don't recognize these tendencies in the current Dream of the Planet, it's usually because we are actively participating in them. We spend our time in gossip and speculation, even competing with each other to dream up the worst possible outcome for any given event. We put fear in charge instead of unconditional love. Throughout history, this habit has amplified the worst human tendencies, even leading to war. Just think of the way that various nations have stockpiled nuclear weapons with the justification that this is necessary to defend against *other* nations with nuclear weapons—a vicious cycle that only creates more fear. On a more basic level, if you spend all day listening to people who think that every inexplicable event has a malevolent hand behind it, you will at some point start to believe that too.

When people talk about overcoming fear, they rarely mention a commitment to abstaining from speculation and gossip. Yet sticking to the facts is an extremely underrated tool for diminishing fear's grip on your mind. If my friend had allowed his imagination to run wild, dreaming up worst-case scenarios about his mother's injuries, he may have been too anxious and overwrought to drive himself to the hospital. By paring things down to the bare facts (his mother had tripped and fallen, and the extent of her injuries was unknown) he avoided giving himself a panic attack and making a difficult situation much worse.

Speculation pulls our minds away from the present moment, into alternate realities which can feel so convincing we often forget they're not real. By refusing to divide our minds between the present moment and these imaginary realities, we can avoid unnecessary fear and drama, and take skillful action whenever it's called for instead of losing our heads.

Slowing Down

Our technologically connected society is the most fast-paced the world has ever seen. We are encouraged to maximize efficiency, get on to the next thing, and pack as much into one day as possible in order to feel we've accomplished "enough." But much like the hamster running on a wheel, few of us ever ask if all this hurry is getting us anywhere.

This urgency typically has a subtle force in the background. Yes, you guessed it: fear. Implicit in the act of hurrying is the fear of "not getting it all done" that few of us ever think to question. This hurry in the mind also affects our bodies, creating physical reactions similar to the fight-or-flight response of increased adrenaline and a faster heart rate. Not only are we taxing our bodies, but we are also taxing our minds, multitasking in an effort to accomplish as much as possible.

The same friend I mentioned earlier in the chapter, who is an experienced meditator, told me about a moment when he was rushing to finish some things at his office one afternoon. A coworker remarked, "What's your hurry?" He replied, "I'm trying to get this done so I can make the evening meditation at the Zen center." Then with some embarrassment, he realized he was "rushing now to meditate later." He then heard his mitote speak up: *See, it's been years and you've made no progress on the spiritual path. Look at you, still rushing to meditate!* Fortunately, he recognized immediately that his mitote was trying to make him feel even worse. Rather than take the bait and beat himself up, he smiled good-naturedly and remembered that the best time to meditate is always now. He slowed down at work and finished his tasks calmly, focusing on being present while doing so.

Fear almost always accompanies urgency. We feel like we need to do something before things get any worse, or before we miss out on an important opportunity. The combination of fear and urgency leads us to make snap decisions that don't take into account possible alternatives or long-term considerations. We take action just to alleviate the anxiety—only to regret our hastiness later. In the current Dream of the Planet, companies profit off this tendency by warning us to "act now" before the opportunity to buy or subscribe is lost forever. In the face of such intense pressure, it takes courage to slow down, come into the present moment, and refuse to hurry.

Excessive hurrying can also cause us to make snap decisions instead of carefully thinking things through, assessing each piece of evidence one at a time. We fall for an alarming news headline without evaluating the merits of its claims; we fail to find our phone or keys within five seconds of looking for them and start telling ourselves they're gone forever. By reclaiming our power of focus, we can eliminate all of this unnecessary stress, bring our bodies and nervous systems to a state of regulation, and reclaim our yes and no when we face urgent demands.

Exercise: Practicing Total Focus

Think of a simple daily task you normally complete in a state of complete or semi-distraction—for example, eating your breakfast or watering your plants.

For the next week, commit to doing this task in a state of full attention. Instead of listening to a podcast, watching TV, or letting your mind wander, bring your focus to the sights, sounds, smells, tastes, and other sensations associated with this task.

Once you've had some practice with a benign task, think of a task which causes you anxiety—for example, giving a presentation or making a difficult phone call. In the hours leading up to this dreaded task, see if you can continue to bring total focus to whatever you are doing, even if your mind is urging you to overthink, speculate, or rehearse. How does it feel to return your focus to the present moment instead of giving in to the anxiety that comes from distraction?

Finally, try to keep this level of focus as you undertake the anxiety-provoking task. Can you stay in the present moment while doing the thing you fear?

Exercise: Owning Your Attention

The modern world is filled with many competing demands for our attention, and the worst culprit is the smartphone that many of us keep on us at all times. Just as we need to define our yes and our no in other areas of our lives, it's important to make conscious choices about our agreements with our phones.

For this exercise, commit to going without your phone for a full day, from the time you wake up until the same time the next morning. (You may need to give some of your friends and family a heads up that you'll be off the grid for a day so no one worries when they don't hear from you.) Notice all the excuses your mind makes to break this commitment. How many of these excuses are based in fear? For example, does your mind tell you that you must have your phone for safety, to keep you from getting lost, or to make sure your loved ones can reach you? Do you fear that you will miss out on interesting experiences and social events, and that this will cause regret or even loss of status? Do you fear the boredom that may arise if you cannot access instant entertainment? Do you fear feelings of emptiness if you can't be completing important tasks all the time?

The next day, allow yourself to use your phone again. Keep paying attention to the thoughts and sensations that cause you to reach for your phone throughout the day. Can you take a breath and make a conscious decision about how you want to respond to those cues? What would it be like to *choose* when and how to use your phone, instead of responding automatically?

If you continue to have trouble with putting down your phone, consider installing one of the apps that will help you limit your use by making certain features, such as social media apps or email, unavailable for set periods of time.

Exercise: Abstaining from Gossip

Most of us habitually engage in some form of gossip, whether that means speculating about another person's relationship or trading notes on political rumors. In this exercise, I invite you to notice what happens in your mind and how you feel when you confine yourself to what you know to be true.

First, make a firm commitment to abstain from gossip for one week and make a plan for how you'll respond when other people invite you to gossip with them. For example, you might say "I don't know too much about that," or "I'd rather not speculate."

The next time someone invites you to gossip, notice what happens in your mind and body. Do you feel a burst of craving, as you would for a dopamine hit? Do you feel disappointment at missing out on a juicy social interaction? What happens to these feelings when you observe them for a few seconds? What does it feel like to listen to other people gossip while you refrain?

Over the course of the week, notice how these feelings change. Do you still feel the craving to gossip on day seven? Or has the prospect become less attractive to you?

Chapter Nine

Acknowledging Past Trauma

Past trauma is often a source of our present fears, which is why any antidote to the poison of fear would be incomplete without a deep examination of the effects of past trauma on our mental and emotional world. If the trauma we experienced was severe, the resulting fears are often very acute, and in those cases the help of a professional therapist or counselor is needed. In other cases, the effects of the trauma can be subtle, especially if we don't recognize our trauma or if we dismiss its effects on us.

For example, a dear friend of mine grew up in a volatile home. His parents were very young when they married, and both had come from family situations where alcohol was abused and domestic altercations were a part of life. His parents continued this cycle early in their marriage, and had many verbal and physical fights when he was a young child. When he was five years old, his parents started going to counseling. Both of them quit drinking, and they turned their lives in the right direction. In fact, my friend has hardly any memory of his earliest years—he just remembers the wonderful childhood he had from age five onward.

Later in life, when he had his first serious relationship in college, he realized that he had a really hard time with conflict and expressing his feelings. When he and his partner would disagree on an important topic, he would shut down emotionally, and end up agreeing to whatever she wanted just to avoid conflict. This would be a recurring pattern in his serious relationships over the next few years. Rather than express his true wishes, he would give in and "keep the peace" at any cost.

It wasn't until his early thirties, when he was married and still repeating the same old patterns, that he got tired of giving in on things that were important to him. He wanted to find a way to speak his truth to his wife, even if it meant that she might strongly disagree or even get upset (at least in his mind). He went to a counselor, who asked him about his childhood. He told the counselor briefly about his parents' early marriage issues, but explained that he had no memory of them as they had worked everything out by the time he was five, and he'd had a very happy childhood generally.

In response, the therapist explained that although he might not remember the fights his parents had when he was a toddler, they had nevertheless left an impression on him. He had probably learned that conflict was scary, and usually resulted in chaos, tears, shouting, and hurt feelings. As a result, he had learned to avoid conflict at all costs—even when it meant backing down on things that were important to him. It was only by getting in touch with the fear he had felt as a young child that my friend could begin to heal his relationship with conflict.

Although most of us are familiar with the concept of childhood trauma, we can also develop trauma from the "normal" demands of adult life. Caring for a sick or dying parent can be traumatic; so can working at a job that exposes you to extreme stress, or trying to support a partner through depression or another mental illness. In my case, I accumulated trauma from caring for my autistic son, whose meltdowns often required me to intervene in ways that were physically and emotionally draining.

One day, my wife and I met up with some friends at Liberty Station, a former naval training center in San Diego that was transformed into a public gathering space filled with art galleries, restaurants, shops, and yoga studios. As we were strolling the grounds, we told our friends about how we'd taken our son and daughter there a couple times. While our daughter loves it, it can be overstimulating for our son, Alejandro. The sounds, people, and lights are way too much for his nervous system, and it overwhelms him to the point where he'll go into fight-or-flight mode. When this happens, we have to leave quickly to help him de-escalate, an experience which can be stressful for all of us.

As we were describing this to our friends, we heard a grunting sound nearby. My wife and I looked at each other, because that sound was very similar to the one our son Alejandro makes when he gets overstimulated—a sound of pain mixed with frustration. Walking closer, we saw that a young man had thrown himself to the ground, and two caring adults were kneeling at his side. Just like our son, he seemed to be having a crisis brought on by the noisy, crowded environment, and his companions were doing their best to calm him.

By the time our son was in his late teens, he was very big and physically strong. If he gets overstimulated, he can be aggressive to the point of self-harm. And if I try to prevent him from hurting himself, he will redirect that aggression toward me. There have been times when I try to restrain him to keep him from hurting himself, he gets even more agitated, and we end up in a terrible struggle. During some of these episodes, I've gotten injured—and it's painful as a parent to feel like I'm increasing my son's suffering even as I'm trying to protect him. The result of this is that I've developed a trauma response around my son's episodes. When I hear that characteristic grunt, my body goes on alert, into the fight-or-flight mode—and this has been going on for several years.

Now, in the food court at Liberty Station, my body and mind began to react as if the boy on the floor were Alejandro, and I had to go help. Of course, it was really a stranger, but my body couldn't tell the difference. Without thinking, I handed the bags I was carrying to my wife.

"Miguel, what are you doing?" she said.

"They might need me," I said.

"Miguel, you don't need to do that," she said. But I was already striding toward the boy and his companions.

I introduced myself and said, "My son has autism. I'm experienced with this. If you need anything, I'm glad to help."

Of course, the adults turned out to be his therapists, and while they thanked me for my thoughtfulness, they assured me they had everything under control. Yet even as I walked back to my wife and our friends, my body was alert and hypervigilant, ready to spring into action. I could feel it in my arms. I could feel it in my legs. I had an overwhelming physical memory of what it was like to restrain an autistic teenager during an episode. Meanwhile, the story machine in my head began to play: *I need to help my son.* And even as I had those thoughts, I was telling myself, *Miguel, that's not your boy.* The protective part of me had been activated, and it took a huge amount of effort to rejoin our group instead of hovering nearby.

We sat at a table, and I kept watching the boy and his therapists out of the corner of my eye. One of the therapists sponged the boy's forehead with a wet rag, and he calmed down enough to let the other therapist slip some noise-cancelling headphones over his ears. Within a few minutes, the boy was laughing and smiling again. He got up as if nothing had happened, and the three of them went on their way. My wife and I looked at each other and both began to cry—because we'd both been on a roller coaster of emotions from the moment we heard that grunt from across the room.

I realized how much more work I still needed to do to recover from my trauma. I couldn't just say, "I don't need therapy, I'm don Miguel Ruiz Jr.!" I couldn't let my pride or my status as an author and nagual stand in the way of my healing. The truth is that I have PTSD and caregiver's fatigue, and I need support. And I'm not afraid to admit that. In addition to drawing on my Toltec spirituality, I also have a therapist I reach out to for help when I need it. And that episode made clear to me that I needed help more than ever.

I am happy to say that my son vastly improved after attending a residential program for young adults with autism. Like many people who have done the work to process and heal from their traumas, he has come home a different person. The healing work he did while in the program gave him more opportunities to enjoy and engage with the beautiful artwork that is life. I can see it in the way he smiles, and he sings so much more than he used to.

I, too, vastly improved through the therapy I received while he was away. Because I did the work to heal, I am able to see and appreciate my son for who he is now, rather than experiencing our relationship through the lens of old wounds and repeating a painful cycle.

If you feel that you might benefit from therapy but are hesitant to try it, I urge you to consider looking for a therapist who's right for you. You might ask trusted friends for recommendations or reach out to practices in your area that seem like they might be a good fit. There is no shame in accepting help, and I personally wish I had sought out support sooner. With that said, there is still plenty you can do on your own, and we'll cover a few basic ways to work through trauma in the sections that follow.

Permission to Heal

Healing from the past is key to experiencing freedom from fear in the present, yet we can only heal from trauma when we give ourselves permission to do so. Granting ourselves permission can often be more difficult than we realize.

Sometimes giving ourselves that permission means setting aside our pride, our self-image, and any other obstacles which may be standing in the way. These obstacles take the form of shoulds and shouldn'ts, similar to what we covered earlier: "The incident happened so many years ago, I should be over it by now," or "What I experienced wasn't that bad; what others went through was far worse and I should be over it by now."

This type of thinking is especially common among adults when they think about the trauma they experienced as children or during their teenage years. We tell ourselves that we "should" be healed already, or that we "shouldn't" need healing at all. These shoulds and shouldn'ts form a fence around our wounds, preventing anyone and anything from getting in.

In order to give yourself permission to heal, you have to begin by acknowledging that the fear and trauma exist in the first place. For many of us, this is surprisingly difficult to do. We don't want to see ourselves as wounded or broken, and so we set the past aside and do our best to downplay our trauma symptoms when they arise. In this way, we live in a state of intellectual denial, even as our bodies and emotions insist on telling the truth.

For a long time, I found it difficult to acknowledge that I had trauma from my son's meltdowns, because I feared it would mean I wasn't doing my job as a father, or that I didn't love him. Yet through clenched muscles and a racing heartbeat, my body never let me forget that it was there.

Our bodies remember so much, even when our minds forget. A friend of mine was born with her umbilical cord wrapped around her neck and almost died. Naturally, she has no conscious memories of this trauma—yet her whole life, she could never stand to have anything remotely close to being wrapped around her neck, including wearing necklaces or shirts with tight collars. When her mother-in-law gave her a fancy choker necklace as a gift, she put it on to be polite, then immediately ran to the bathroom and vomited out of sheer panic. Even though she couldn't remember it, the memory of nearly being strangled to death was still present in her body. To me, this story is a powerful example of the fact that we are more than our conscious minds. Our bodies, too, are storehouses of memory, and they can show us where we need to heal if we listen to them.

In many cases, healing past trauma means engaging in a process of forgiveness: whether that's forgiving another person, forgiving yourself, or forgiving life itself—what some might call forgiving God. The first step to forgiveness is often accepting the past exactly as it is and acknowledging the truth of what happened and how it affected us, no matter how painful it may be. Although we may want to believe that we are unscathed by the events we lived through, this is rarely the case—and simply acknowledging that fact is the first step to healing.

Fear and Respect

Healing from past trauma often means making a transition from fearing something to respecting it. My dear friend HeatherAsh Amara, a fellow author and a nagual who studied under my father and grandmother, tells a wonderful story about this in her book *The Warrior Goddess Way*.

While living in Northern California, she had a close encounter with a patch of poison oak that left her itchy and miserable for more than week. Just like that, the magical landscape she'd loved was transformed into a place of danger, with menacing plants lurking under every tree. Not only that, but friends and acquaintances warned her that repeat occurrences would be even worse, making it imperative that she avoid poison oak at all costs.

HeatherAsh soon realized that her enjoyment of the land where she lived had been completely poisoned by fear. She had become hypervigilant, scanning the landscape for threats instead of relishing its beauty, and she even stopped petting her beloved dogs in case they carried some of the dreaded substance on their fur.

Then one day, she decided that enough was enough. She found a stand of poison oak and sat down in front of it. Gazing at its beautiful leaves, she asked, "How can I release my fear of you?" The answer that came to her was one word: respect.

Respect and fear have a lot in common. When you respect something, you might keep a healthy distance from it. For example, even professional surfers know that respecting the sea means staying out of it when the waves are too big. This isn't the same as *fearing* the ocean. Respect means developing your knowledge and understanding so you can make wise choices, as opposed to the helter-skelter reactions that arise out of fear.

Respect also involves self-knowledge. It means asking yourself questions like, *How much can I handle?* and being honest about the answers. An experienced surfer can go out in conditions which would not be appropriate for a beginner, while maintaining their respect for the ocean. For HeatherAsh, respecting poison oak meant taking simple measures like wearing long pants outdoors, while trusting that she had the natural alertness not to blunder into a sprawling patch unawares. She could therefore respect poison oak instead of fearing it.

In my own life, I've found that I need to respect the trauma I have around my son's meltdowns. I can't just pretend my PTSD symptoms don't exist or aren't happening; I can't just say "I'll handle it," and run blindly into ten-foot waves that are going to pound me into the sand. I don't live in fear of my PTSD, but I do respect it by knowing my limits, taking steps to support myself, and being honest about what I'm going through. Fear closes down possibilities, while respect helps us see creative solutions—and when you make that transition from fear to respect, everything changes.

Healing Through Exposure

Many people know that before he became a Toltec teacher, my father was in a car accident in which he almost died. What they don't know is that minutes after he was discharged from the hospital, my uncle and grandmother handed him the car keys and informed him that *he* would be driving them home from Cuernavaca to Mexico City—a distance of about sixty miles. They knew that if my father drove a car again right away, there was less of a chance for fear and avoidance to take hold.

When my father became a parent, he used the same philosophy with me and my brothers. If any of us ever told my dad or grandmother that we were afraid of something—for example, spiders or heights or giving a speech—they would find a way to make sure that we faced those things as soon as possible. Naturally, we soon learned to keep quiet if we were scared of something! But the truth is, the times when my dad tricked one of us into speaking in front of an audience or going into a dark cave, we always ended up better for it. Far from traumatizing us, we learned again and again that we were stronger than our fears.

Of course, if the situation ever got too intense, we knew we had the option of saying no. My father and grandmother never teased us or shamed us when we were afraid. Instead, they created situations where we had the opportunity to flourish, and they understood that this didn't always happen on the first try. When fear took hold, they would encourage us to pause and allow the emotion to flow through us like a wave. Once that wave crests and you catch your breath, you can look up and ask yourself, *What do I want to do?* You can make a conscious choice instead of letting the fear instinct decide on your behalf.

A few years ago, I was trying to keep my son from hurting himself when I fell and got a concussion. As part of my recovery, my doctor recommended music therapy. It turns out that doing two things at once, such as singing and playing guitar, encourages different parts of the brain to work together, and this is exactly what I needed to heal. I already played a little guitar, so I began to take singing lessons from my cousin Dina.

After we'd been working together for a little while, one of the homework assignments she gave me was to sing with a group of mariachis. "Dina, don't make me do that," I begged her. "They're professional musicians." I thought of how painful it would be for the mariachis to hear me yodeling over their music like a drowned cat. But Dina insisted. "This is the only way you're going to push yourself to the next level," she said. "I've seen it a thousand times."

At the end of our next power journey in Teotihuacan, my friend Alberto arranged for some mariachis to come play. I'd been practicing a José Alfredo Jiménez song called "Ella," which I was now going to sing. With my brothers and cousins looking on, the mariachis began to play. I took a deep breath and began to sing. To my surprise, I felt a surge of excitement. It reminded me of performing with the choir when I was in high school.

A moment or two later, I stumbled. I realized the mariachis were playing in a different key than the one in which I'd been practicing. For a few seconds, my excitement turned to dread as I hunted among all the different instruments for one thread that I could recognize and follow. My voice wavered. *Oh no,* I thought. *I have absolutely no idea where I am.*

Luckily, the mariachi playing guitar caught my eye. I locked onto the familiar chord progression, and within a few seconds I'd found my place again. Afterward, my cousin was ecstatic. "Miguel," she said, "don't worry about the mistakes. We can always work on those later. The important thing is that you've made it to the next level. So many of my students are too afraid to even try!"

A few months later, I was in the San Diego airport when I came across a grand piano they'd placed there for travelers to play. Without hesitating, I slid off my backpack, sat down, and played "Ella." Just like with the mariachis, I felt an unexpected flood of joy shining through my nervousness. It felt like the joy was waiting for me just beyond my fear, the way the sun can be hidden behind a thin layer of clouds. In that moment, I truly understood what the voices in my mitote were robbing from me when they told me I wasn't "good enough" to play and sing where other people could hear—and I realized I always had the option of choosing another way.

Our fear is not an end point, but a jumping-off point for unimaginable growth. Learn to see your fear as the seed of something incredible, and you will unlock the secret of life.

Exercise: Reassessing Your Fears

When you've lived through a traumatic event, it can lead you to make broad generalizations about people and situations. For example, if you were attacked by a dog, you might conclude that all dogs are dangerous at all times, and go to great lengths to avoid them. You might form some rigid and unfair beliefs, such as the following: "I would be powerless in the event of an attack"; "people who own dogs have no care for others' safety"; or even "I can't be friends with anyone who owns a dog." In this exercise, I invite you to consciously revisit these kinds of assumptions.

First, think of a traumatic event that continues to affect you to this day. Now, make a list of all the beliefs and agreements you've formed as a result of this event. Give yourself time to fully explore this question—chances are you will find more items for this list than you expected.

Now, think of all the resources that are available to you now that were not available to you at the time of the traumatic incident. Do you have more knowledge and awareness than before? Are you bigger and stronger? Do you have new tools or skills that you didn't have before? What about social resources like a protective partner, family, neighbors, and friends? What about environmental, social, and political conditions—have they changed, too?

Next, revisit your list of beliefs. Go through the list, and update these beliefs to reflect your current situation and newfound strengths. For example, you might write, "Some dogs are dangerous, but many are friendly—and I have the skills to tell the difference."

How does it feel to realize that you are not the same person you were at the time of the traumatic incident? Not only that, but neither is anyone else. The world has changed since that formative event, and so have you.

Exercise: Draining a Memory of Its Charge

As an adult, you've probably experienced trauma or grief and the various stages that play out after the occurrences of such an event. In the immediate aftermath, you probably can't talk about the thing without breaking down. After some time has passed, you might feel overcome with emotion intermittently as the event pops into your mind. After years, you may be able to discuss that time in a more detached way. You've had a chance to synthesize a lot of thoughts and feelings over the years, and you've reached some conclusions and maybe some level of resolution. Even if you never speak publicly about your trauma, you can tell you've put trauma behind you when you can talk about it without getting disturbed or upset—in other words, when you've drained the memory of its charge. In this exercise, I offer one such tool for doing this.

First, call to mind a positive memory—a time when you felt happy, safe, and loved. Imagine these positive feelings in detail, until your body feels warm and relaxed and your mind feels bright and at peace.

Once you have established this positive, luminous state, call to mind a traumatic memory. For now, start with a minor trauma. Imagine that your traumatic memory is a ball you are holding in your hands—perhaps the size of a tennis ball. This memory, as bad as it may be, is not big enough to impact the happy, safe, loving feelings in your body at this moment. Hold the ball for a few minutes while staying connected to the positive feelings in your body and mind. When you are ready, toss the ball back to wherever it came from, knowing that you can always return to it again.

When you repeat this practice on a regular basis, your brain learns that you can revisit this traumatic memory from a place of total safety. Over time, the fearful charge associated with this memory will diminish as you train yourself to connect with the feelings of safety instead.

Exercise: Reaching Beyond Fear

Many of us turn back at the first sign of fear, as if the presence of fear is a definite sign that something terrible is about to happen. Yet often, a twinge of fear can be present when something *wonderful* is about to happen. For example, the fear we feel when we are invited to sing, dance, or speak our truth isn't a sign that we are in any physical danger, just that we're getting ready to step outside our comfort zone. In this exercise, I invite you to discover this truth for yourself.

First, think of an activity you loved as a child, such as singing, dancing, drawing, or acting, but which you have stopped doing in public because you're "no good at it" or because you feel that twinge of fear that people will laugh. At some point in the next week, make a point of doing this exact thing in public. This might mean singing a song at your friend's birthday party, dancing at your local salsa night, or taking your art supplies to the coffee shop.

How does it feel to rebel against the rules laid down by your mitote? Do the people around you open up and express more joy when they see you rebelling against your own fear? What does it mean that we can be afraid of completely wonderful things, not just objectively fearful things?

Chapter Ten

Letting Go

My Uncle Duke was born in 1953 in South Vietnam. When the Vietnam War broke out in the 1960s, he was just a teenager. Still, he enlisted as a soldier, just like many of his schoolmates. Early in the war, he got shot and was badly injured, but after the army patched him up they sent him right back into combat. He soon took another bullet; they patched him up a second time and sent him back into combat *again*. When South Vietnam lost the Civil War, Uncle Duke came to the United States as a refugee—first to Pennsylvania and eventually to San Diego, California. That was where he met my aunt, fell in love with her, and became my uncle.

In Vietnam, Uncle Duke had trained as a mechanic, so he opened an automotive shop in El Cajon, California, which he ran for many years. Then one day, a customer walked into his shop and found him unconscious on the floor. Nobody knew what had happened to him—we wondered if he had tripped and fallen, or if someone had hit him on the head. After paramedics rushed him to the ER, doctors told us that his brain had begun to swell. By the end of the day, he was brain-dead. Uncle Duke had told my aunt that he never wanted to be placed on life support, so even though she was in a state of shock and bewilderment, she signed the papers instructing the doctors to unhook him from the machines. Then she asked my mother and me if we would like to sit next to Uncle Duke while he passed away.

In my family's tradition, we have a ceremony we call the Last Communion, in which we honor a person whose human life is coming to an end. In order to prepare ourselves for this ceremony, we first have to let our emotions flow—because once the ceremony begins, it's not about us anymore, it's about the person dying. My mother, my aunt, my cousins, and I stood outside Uncle Duke's room for a moment, letting ourselves feel all the shock, sorrow, and fear that was inside of us. We cried and hugged each other, recognizing the truth of our feelings without suppressing anything.

When we were ready, we walked into the room where Uncle Duke was lying. My aunt held one of his hands and I held the other one, with my mother sitting by his legs. As Uncle Duke faded from this life, we told stories about who he was and shared our memories of him. My uncle was a mechanic and a Vietnam War veteran, and built like a brick of a man. But he also loved ballroom dancing. He loved to dance the cha-cha and the tango, and he even opened his own dance studio with my aunt. As we spoke, we kept our total focus on Uncle

Duke, surrounding him in the loving web of our attention. I was holding his hand, and even though he was unconscious, I could feel his presence. He was alive.

Then, all at once, I realized that Uncle Duke's spirit had left his body. Just like that, I felt his presence had disappeared from the room. I didn't need to hear the heart monitor. I didn't even need to hear his last breath. I could feel it in his hand that he was no longer there.

Within seconds, the warmth in his hand had disappeared and his fingers had become perceptibly more rigid. I went from holding the hand of a living being to holding an inanimate object, like a mannequin with skin. And this experience taught me one of the biggest lessons of my life, a lesson that my father and grandmother had been trying to teach me for years: I am not this body.

Even though I'd long had an intellectual grasp of this concept, this moment was the first time I experienced its truth on a level deeper than my mind. Suddenly it became clear to me that while my uncle's body was still there, he was not. I was holding his hand, but there was no life inside that hand anymore. His body, which had seemed so much like *him*, was an empty husk, a collection of pipes and wires that allowed him to move and talk. Without his nagual, it was nothing.

Even though my family's Toltec tradition is indigenous in origin, we also embrace the truths of Western science. As I reflected on my Uncle Duke's passing, two lessons from physics came to mind. The first is that energy can never be destroyed, it can only be transformed. And the second is that in order for an object to move, there needs to be a force that moves the object. As my Toltec ancestors would say, you need the nagual for the tonal to move—where *nagual* means spirit, and *tonal* means physical matter. My body is matter, *tonal*. But I am not the tonal. I am the nagual who moves it. You might know the nagual as spirit, you might know it as soul, you might know it as light, intent, God.

Whatever your tradition calls it, that's the energy that moves the body—and when you watch it leave, it becomes a powerful teacher.

After witnessing my uncle's death, I found that my own fear of death diminished markedly. Of course, that doesn't mean I don't take precautions to protect my health, nor am I in any rush to leave—just that the physical transition itself had ceased to scare me. It was clear to me that Uncle Duke's energy had simply withdrawn from his body, the way electricity withdraws from a lamp when you unplug it.

I remember the time I asked my father where we go when we die. By that point, he had been through more than one near-death experience—the car crash in which he saw himself exiting the vehicle and pulling all of his friends to safety, and the massive heart attack that left him in a coma. I knew that his perspective on death would go beyond conventional theories about the afterlife.

He told me to imagine that I'd lived my whole life from the point of view of a single drop of water. Everything I can see, hear, taste, and feel is confined to that drop of water, and I believe that this constitutes all of reality. "Now," he said, "imagine that at the moment of your last breath, your perception expands to the whole ocean."

I don't know where we go when we die. But what I do know is this: at this very moment, I am alive. And as long as the nagual is contained within my body, my hands can type these words. The moment the nagual leaves me, those same hands will become inanimate objects—but that doesn't mean the nagual has ceased to exist, any more than the sun ceases to exist when it goes behind the clouds.

Fear of bodily death is one thing that the vast majority of humans have in common. From a biological standpoint, all living creatures are programmed to fear death in the physical sense and take steps to avoid it. In this way, the fear of death is healthy and protective, and exists for a good reason.

But fear of death is also psychological, and can get out of hand when it dominates our minds, causing us emotional pain and anxiety that make it difficult to make good use of the time we are alive. By confronting this fear, we not only expand our awareness and knowledge—we also heighten our empathy for others who are dealing with these same fears.

Letting Your Stories Die

Psychological fear of death becomes acute when we become attached to the story of our lives instead of remembering that we are life itself. The story of your life is just that: a story. When the story of your life is created with the love of an artist and then let go at a moment's notice, then the story becomes a masterpiece. It is your *attachment* to the story that brings the fear of death.

Think of who you were at age four. Maybe you loved certain books and toys; you probably had different friends, cared about different things, and had very different stories about your life than the ones you have now. At some point, your four-year-old self changed their story. And that's a good thing—if you'd clung to that four-year-old's story or identity, people would think you were crazy. The same is true for your identity as a twelve-year-old, a twenty-year-old, and every passing decade after that. If you look at things this way, you will soon realize that you have already died many times, in the sense that you have given up a story or identity that once felt like the whole truth of who you were in order to step into a new story or identity—in order to evolve.

If I told you that when you wake up tomorrow morning, you will be twenty years older than you are today, you might feel a sense of shock, grief, and fear similar to what many of us feel when we think about death. It's too great a leap; there are too many unknowns, and not enough time to wrap up all the loose ends of *this* life. You might protest that you're not ready. Yet most of you reading this book have already lived to be twenty years older than you once were, and will live to be twenty years older than you are now, with all the change, loss, and uncertainty that entails. Clearly, we are much greater than we realize—and keeping this awareness at the front of our minds can greatly reduce our fear of death, and indeed, reduce our fear around any type of ending, real or imagined.

New Life for the Nagual

Every moment of every day, we are surrounded by endings—moments when the nagual moves from one state of being to another. Water evaporates from a puddle, leaving behind dry ground. The cereal in your bowl becomes the energy in your body. The fly who buzzed around your kitchen for days shows up as a weightless corpse on the windowsill. Bodily death isn't rare and exceptional, but constant and necessary.

When a person dies, we often say that their spirit lives on in various ways: through their children, their friends and loved ones, the things they created, the ideas they shared, and the institutions on which they made a mark. This isn't just a figure of speech. Throughout our lives, we literally set things into motion: we are the force behind the object, the nagual behind the tonal. Once we set those things into motion, the energy we put into them doesn't disappear. Instead, it travels forward in ways that we can't always follow. Sometimes, it is only when a person dies that we discover just how much they set into motion—often, more than they themselves realized.

Of course, knowing this doesn't necessarily ease our grief when we've lost a loved one, and it may be of little comfort when faced with the possibility of losing our own life sooner than we had hoped or planned. The problem isn't in the grieving—most animals grieve—but in the obsessive worrying that can accompany the prospect of death.

In Western culture, life and death are typically thought of as opposites, like light and dark, hot and cold, and up and down. My family's Toltec tradition has a different take. We teach that life and death are not opposites—life has no opposite. Rather, birth and death are opposites.

Like the drop of water entering the ocean, bodily death means the nagual in us loses its sense of separation. The unique perspective is gone, but the experience is now universal. The death of a physical form allows the nagual to continue its journey through the endless dance of life. Although we may yearn to know exactly where our loved one is, or what we will become after death, I have a feeling these questions become meaningless the moment our individual droplet of water merges with the great ocean, and we lose all identification with the stories that once defined us.

Exercise: Stalking Death

While we are quite good at blocking it out, death is in fact all around us, all the time, in one form or another. In this exercise, I invite you to heighten your awareness of this fundamental truth, with the goal of observing how the nagual is neither created nor destroyed.

For one twenty-four-hour period, take note of all the endings you observe. This might include literal death, such as insects or plants dying, or smaller deaths such as the end of a day, the end of a piece of music, or the end of a meal.

At the same time, observe small instances of death within your own body: a hair or eyelash falling out, nails needing a trim, urine and feces carrying away the remnants of the food and water you consume, the energy of the day giving way to an intense desire for sleep.

How much fear do you attach to these small, everyday deaths? Does your fear of "big" death change as you pay attention to all the smaller deaths you encounter regularly?

Exercise: Leaving Your Legacy

We can diminish our fear of death by putting positive things in motion during our life. In this exercise,

I invite you to reflect on the ways you can use your nagual to shape the tonal during this lifetime.

First, ask yourself what you would like to be remembered for after you die. Being a steady and dependable presence in your loved ones' lives? Creating a beautiful and enduring work of art? Preserving the environment? Founding a movement? Think of all the ways you've already begun to set this vision into motion. What are you *already doing* to achieve this goal?

Then write down three things you will do in the next year to further this vision. How does it feel to set an intention for the remaining time your nagual is animating this body, instead of leaving it undefined?

Exercise: Letting-Go Meditation

Death means letting go—both of your physical body and of the stories you have about who you are. Whether you've given it much thought or not, chances are you've already done some version of this process many times over the course of growing older. In this meditation, I invite you to reflect on these constant cycles.

Sit in a comfortable position where you won't be disturbed for ten or fifteen minutes. Close your eyes, and breathe normally.

First, picture yourself as a newborn. Realize that the body you had then is forever lost to you—you will never get it back. The world you inhabited as a newborn is also gone forever.

Now, call up an image of yourself as a three- or four-year-old. As before, remember that the body you had then has already "died"—you will never inhabit that particular body again.

Repeat this process for as many ages as you like. Consider that even though you never buried these bodies or held a funeral, you nevertheless let go of them—otherwise you would never have grown into the person you are now. What does it feel like to reflect on the fact that you have already lost the person you thought you were many times over?

Letting Go

Conclusion

When my brother and I take apprentices on power journeys in Teotihuacan, one of the places we visit is the Plaza of Hell—a wide, flat expanse at the base of the Pyramid of Quetzalcoatl, which can get unbearably hot and bright at midday. In the Toltec tradition, the Plaza of Hell represents the mind in turmoil: specifically, the psychological fears that can proliferate as a result of our domestication, and which are endlessly echoed by the mitote.

Sometimes when Jose and I guide apprentices through the Plaza of Hell, we end with a ritual in which they feed their fears to Quetzalcoatl, the huge stone snake at the base of the pyramid. Our fears can often feel like they're too big for us to handle—but they're nothing to a dragon. It's always moving to see how relieved the apprentices look after symbolically handing over their deepest anxieties to this massive, powerful figure.

Many times, what we really need to move past our fears is to call on something bigger than ourselves, whether that's God, the universe, or a huge stone carving of a feathered serpent, and to say, "Here, take this—I can't carry it on my own."

The moments in which we surrender are often the moments in which our deepest strengths are revealed to us. It's almost like the dragon turns to us and says, "You were afraid of *that*? Really? I can burn this thing up, no problem." In some cases, when you gaze into the dragon's eyes, you might have a moment of recognition, and realize the dragon is you!

When we let go of our psychological fears, or burn them up with the dragon's breath, we redeem our own beauty, our own intelligence, and our incredible powers of creation. When we cast the poisoned arrow aside and see it for what it really is, we can finally say, *Forgive me, mind, I didn't know what I was doing. I used you as an instrument of my own enslavement. I used you to subjugate myself. You are now relieved of the duty of replaying my fears over and over again, and of holding on to the past.* With the poisoned arrow safely removed, we can instead tell our minds, *I have an assignment for you. Will you be my ally? Will you be the instrument that allows me not just to navigate this world, but to see life as it is? Would you be the voice of unconditional love in my life? Would you help me grow in temachia?*

Feel the space you occupy on this earth, the blood in your veins, and the air in your lungs. One day, this communion will no longer be. One day, your body is going to die. But that day is not today. Today, you are alive. Today, you are breathing. You are infinite potential because you are alive. And at this moment, you can choose to create the life you want to live—a life rooted in personal freedom and unconditional love, the antidote to any poisoned arrow that comes your way.

Acknowledgments

It is my great honor to acknowledge my teachers in the Toltec Tradition: my grandmother, Madre Sarita; my father, don Miguel Ruiz; my mother, doña Coco; my uncle, Dr. J. L. Ruiz; and my brothers, don Jose Ruiz and don Leonardo Ruiz. Thank you for teaching me that love is the perfect balance between generosity and gratitude.

I want to acknowledge my family: Susan, Alejandro, and Audrey. Your love is my joy, it makes me so happy to have you in my life. For everything that happens in life, I will always love you.

I want to acknowledge my Ink Brother, my publisher and editor, Randy of Hierophant Publishing! Thank you so much for once again giving me the opportunity to share my family's tradition with everyone, and for working with me on the creation of this book while I went through my journey of healing. I know this book will help everyone who reads it. Thank you!

I want to acknowledge the Hierophant editorial team of Hilary, Susie, and Grace. Thank you for putting order to my thoughts in a way that everyone can understand. The book is wonderful—thank you for making it so. Muchas gracias.

I want to acknowledge everyone who helped me in my journey of healing: Rick Ivone Jr., Mary Tuton, Dr. D. Emina, Dr. C. Ruiz, Dr. A. Ruiz, Dr. J. Pelayo-Garcia, Dr. M. Macias, Dr. K. Loharun, K. Delgadillo, and Dr. B. Drain. Thank you all so much for helping me heal. I am forever grateful to you all.

Finally, I want to acknowledge the Ruiz Team: Karla Ruiz, Aaron Landman, and Natalie Gil Eklof. Your hard work and dedication have allowed us to reach incredible heights. Thank you for everything you do.

About the Author

Don Miguel Ruiz Jr. is a nagual, a Toltec master of transformation. He is the internationally bestselling author of *The Mastery of Self*, *The Mastery of Life*, *The Five Levels of Attachment*, *Don Miguel Ruiz's Little Book of Wisdom*, and *Living a Life of Awareness*, and the coauthor (with HeatherAsh Amara) of *The Seven Secrets to Healthy, Happy Relationships*. A direct descendant of the Toltecs of the Eagle Knight lineage, he is the son of don Miguel Ruiz, author of *The Four Agreements*. By combining the wisdom of his family's tradition with the knowledge gained from his own personal journey, he now helps others realize their own path to personal freedom. Visit him at *www.miguelruizjr.com*.

San Antonio, TX
www.hierophantpublishing.com